Disclaimer

This book is written with the understanding that the author was not engaged in rendering legal services. The information included has been carefully prepared and is correct to the best of his knowledge as of the publication date. If you require legal or expert advice, the services of professionals should be used. The author disclaims any personal liability, either directly or indirectly, for advice or information presented in this book.

The information as described has been used successfully to obtain profitable business for some of the persons who have used it. Although all efforts have been expended to supply the latest in complete, accurate and up-to-date information, it must be understood that the ultimate success of the user is dependent upon market conditions, efforts expended by the user, and other variable factors that are beyond the control of the authors, and that neither the users' actual expenses nor profits are guaranteed nor implied.

Throughout this book, trademarked names are used. Rather than put a trademark symbol after every occurrence of the trademarked name, we used the names in an editorial fashion only, and to the benefit of the trademark owner, with no intention of infringement of the trademark.

At the time this edition was printed and released, all of the sites listed were active and accessible to anyone having access to the Internet. Neither the author nor the publisher is responsible for broken links, abandoned sites, or changes that are beyond their control.

Table of Contents

Chapter 1 – General Stuff

For all of its size, power, interaction, and influence on today's world, the Internet is a rather simplistic concept and the web, a sub-element of the Internet, is even simpler in concept.

By strict definition, the Internet is a communications system that comprises every computer in the world that is able to link to the telephone system (a generic definition) to send and receive messages to any other computer that is connected to the telephone system.

Since this definition includes fax machines, remote control devices, and computers that are specifically designed to talk to each other, the definition has to be modified a bit.

The current definition of the Internet, therefore, is as follows:

The Internet is a communications system that comprises every computer device in the world that is able to link to the telephone system via an Internet Service Provider (ISP). It runs software specifically designated as Internet tools, to send and receive messages to any other computer that is connected to the telephone system and that uses those same Internet tools.

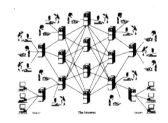

The Internet started with a system called the ARPANET, a simplistic project to allow the super computers of days gone by at universities and colleges to share their knowledge bases with each other.

The storage sites were, and are still, called gopher sites or gopher holes. They are enormous compendiums of research and academic information that is still being added to and which is available for usage by anybody, anywhere, since it is public domain information and copyright FREE.

When personal computers entered the public eye in the early 1980s, devoted enthusiasts of computers and other special interests began to use the Internet concept (computers talking to computers via the phone lines) to communicate with other enthusiasts. These became known as SIGs or special interest groups.

BACKGROUND OF THE WEB

Just for purposes of review, remember that the Internet is simply a lot of computers that can talk to each other. They use the phone line systems, cable systems, fiber optics, and microwave systems to achieve this.

Within this enormous complex of computers lies a system known as the World Wide Web or simply the web.

The web, for all practical purposes, is a gigantic library of stored information that exists within the Internet complex and can be accessed by anyone who has a connection through the Internet itself.

Since the web is a gigantic library, this means that a web site is the electronic equivalent of a book. To exemplify this, think about what you find in a regular library: books, tapes, audios, videos, pricelists, catalogs, etc.

What do we find on the web? The same stuff!

According to Google, this enormous electronic library currently has in excess of 50 billion pages. This number varies depending on whose statistics you believe but regardless of which ones you decide to believe, the web is currently an enormous library and is getting bigger by millions of pages each day.

Before we proceed we need to define a few technical terms, not to make a genuine techno-geek out of you, but so that you understand the current vocabulary of the web and its design.

1. The web is a gigantic library.

2. A web site is electronic book.

3. The person creating the web site is the author.

4. The person visiting the web site is the reader—sometimes known as the client.

5. The server is electronic bookshelf where our web site is stored so that visitors have immediate access.

6. The home page is the starting or entry point into a site and the electronic equivalent of the cover of the book.

The net versus the web. In order to understand the realities of the web, we have to look at the fact that the Internet, which is the environment in which you're actually operating, was developed and exists today to send and receive text-based information only. If you remember the old green screen monitors where we had nothing but text and the blinking cursor on the screen, that's all the Internet can do today.

The problem was, and is, that as users of the Internet we wanted more than just text. We wanted graphics, multimedia and hypertext linking, so the engineers created a system that we know today as the web.

Simply put, when information is stored on a web site it is converted to a text-based code called HTML. When a user requests a download and it arrives at their computer, the browser software (which is in actuality a translator) converts the HTML code into pictures and sounds that we can see and hear.

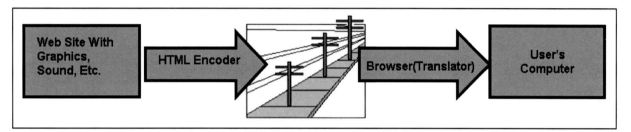

This is how we get all of this delightful multimedia content out of a text-only system.

For as wonderful as this is, it does suffer from what we call a double translation problem which results in time delays, because the system has to encode it into HTML send it down a transmission system like the phone line system, and then decode and redisplays it on your computer. It works but it's time consuming.

For it is dynamic and dramatic as the graphics conversion and browser system is, the real power tool of the web is its ability to hypertext link.

As you cruise through a page full of black text on your monitor and encounter colored text that's underlined (www.RoundsMiller.com), you know that you found a hypertext link and clicking on it will take you anywhere in the world where the programmer has decided you should go.

From a web development standpoint, it's a very simple tool to use because all you have to do is highlight the word or words that you want to turn into a hyperlink, hit the right mouse button, and select *hyperlink*.

At this point you simply type in the forwarding address and when you strike the return key, you will have automatically programmed a hyperlink that will take the visitor anywhere in the world by simply clicking on the link. (Oh yes, you can make a graphic object a hyperlink the same way—just select it with your mouse, right click, add the hyperlink, and it'll become a portal to wherever you designate the forward address.)

THE FOUR PROTOCOLS OF THE INTERNET

It's vital that you realize that the web is not a separate system, but one of the four protocols of the Internet.

The Internet we know and use evolved as a result of three technologies that was around in a hobby or amateur state before the professional tool that we know as the web was developed.

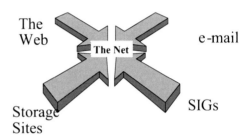

The Four Protocols of the Internet

E-mail: The first thing that was developed was e-mail or electronic mail. In its early versions, it was almost exclusively text because that's the way the original system was configured.

SIGs: As more and more people began to use e-mail to communicate with each other, they discovered that they had common interests, and discussion groups or SIGS (special interest groups) popped up. Ironically it was one of these special interest groups called the USENET newsgroups that were probably the most influential element in the explosive growth of the Internet.

Storage Sites: Prior to the web and the technology that we use today for e-mail, it was very difficult to send attachments such as software, video, audio, and photos along with e-mail. Storage sites or remote storage lockers were developed as a technique for storing and retrieving information.

The Web: Then came the web, dedicated portion of the Internet that currently incorporates the best features of just about everything that we've ever come up with plus a lot of its own, and that's what we're talking about in this book.

BANDWIDTH

First of all we need to explain what bandwidth is. This is a technical term which loosely translated means delivery speed and the best way to exemplify this is to think of a fire hose and a garden hose.

A fire hose is about a foot in diameter while a garden hose is only about an inch in diameter. If you were to pump water through both hoses for a minute, you would get a lot more water through the fire hose than you would through the garden hose.

In the world of water delivery, the fire hose would be considered a high-bandwidth delivery device and the garden hose would be considered a low-bandwidth delivery device.

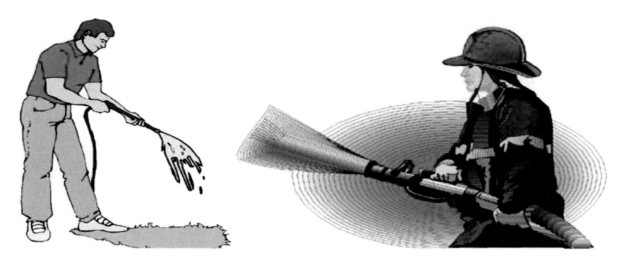

In the world of the Internet we're dealing with electronic signals and the signals are carried through different kinds of electrical conductors. The oldest and most common of these are the copper telephone wires that were installed back when we had analog rotary dial phones.

These are what the phone company calls POTS which stands for *plain old telephone service* and although you've probably been using a touch tone phone for a long time, most of the cables especially in older residential areas, are still the analog POTS configuration that were installed back when we used to dial the phone and had party lines.

These POTS lines are rather slow and are called low-bandwidth lines.

High-bandwidth lines are DSL, cable, fiber optics, and microwave. These are the functional equivalent of the fire hose and they can deliver a lot of information in a short time.

The problems that we run into because of POTS lines have to do with who still uses POTS lines.

According to the current US web statistics, about 90 percent of the US businesses have high-bandwidth connections but only about 60 percent of the homes have high-bandwidth connections. Most of them are still using dial-up POTS lines.

The reasons for this are many and varied but it mostly has to do with economics and the availability of phone lines in the homes. The significance of this has to do with what you, as the web site supplier, have on your web site.

If you are putting a lot of high-volume material, such as photographs, audio, video, and are delivering it to a business, the chances are that they have a high-speed line and these big files will download very fast, without any problems.

If, conversely, you are delivering the same high-volume content to homes, you've got four chances in ten of having a slow speed connection and the material that you're supplying from your web site will slowly creep down the screen.

Although it's delivered eventually, it's very aggravating and causes people in many cases to simply click off the site.

Later in the book we're going to show you several *workarounds* that will help you with the problem of people having to use POTS lines. Please consider these workarounds very carefully because when people become aggravated they click off your site and that won't do you any good.

Some more terminology you'll need to know. Although we're still not trying to make technology gurus out of you, you will need a few more technical terms that are used when creating web sites and working with the Internet in general.

Most of these have been around since the creation of the Internet but many of them are still misunderstood by the users of the Internet.

ISP (Internet Service Provider): you've undoubtedly heard the Internet called the information superhighway. Think of the ISP as a tollgate where for a certain amount of money each month they give us access off and on the information superhighway. These include suppliers like AOL, MSN, the phone company, and your cable providers.

ISP host: these are service providers who, for a fee, will rent us a certain amount of server space or electronic library shelf space each month to place our web site.

Upload: When we send information from our computer to any computer on the Internet it's called an upload.

Download: When we retrieve information from the Internet and bring it to our computer is called a download. It doesn't make any difference whether we read it, print it, save it, or forward it; it's still called a download.

Search engine: the devices that we use to locate information on the web.

Client: This is the person who visits our web site. Sometimes they are known as the visitor or the customer.

Browser: One of the oldest terms on the Internet is browser and it's still grossly misunderstood. The name would lead you to believe that it browses and looks for things on the Internet. Nothing could be further from the truth because the tool that does this is the search engine.

The browser should be renamed translator because its primary function is to translate the coded information that arrives in our computer from the Internet into things that we can see and hear.

The most popular browser in the world is Microsoft's Internet Explorer but there are several others available including Netscape Navigator, Mozilla, Opera, FireFox and a host of new ones. The choice of browser is up to you and they all do the same thing albeit a little differently.

Authoring software: this is the software that we use to create the web site on our computer. For all practical purposes it's desktop publishing software on steroids because once we've created the web site in a format and layout that we're happy with, the software automatically writes the computer code needed to post it on the web.

HTML: This is the computer language of the web. It stands for hypertext markup language. In today's progressive software development world, it's rarely necessary for anybody who creates a web site to study or understand the HTML code because the authoring software automatically writes it for you.

As a general rule, the only time that you, as the web site developer, will be required to use the HTML code, is when you add a meta tag or electronic search links to your site. Other than that, you should never have to worry about HTML code other than that it is the actual language of the web itself.

Cyberspace: this is a term borrowed from in 1984 science fiction novel called the Neuromancer and it's simply a generic term used to describe that ethereal place where things happen on the Internet. It's the technical equivalent of *out there somewhere* and although it's widely used, the truth is that most people really don't know where things are stored when they talk about cyberspace.

Since the Internet is a lot of computers that can talk to each other, it's possible, and highly likely, that the information is stored on several computers and the truth is that nobody knows exactly where it's at.

For all practical purposes, it doesn't make any difference where it's at as long as you have access to it.

Snail mail: This is the generic term that we use to describe any physically delivered mail including US mail, UPS, FedEx, or DHL.

Web: The entire electronic library of stored information.

Web site: A group of information equivalent to a book or catalog.

Web page: Any page of information on the web itself.

Home page: The web's equivalent of a book cover. The home page is where visitors normally enter the web site. A home page is a web pages but not all web pages are a home page.

Nothing is free: Although a lot of goods and services are offered as free on the Internet, the truth is that nothing is free, just like there is no such thing as a free lunch. Whenever something is offered for free on the Internet, you will most likely be paying for it by accepting advertising or providing targeted demographic information for future marketing solicitations.

CONSIDERATIONS WHEN DEVELOPING YOUR WEB SITE

Never forget that you just one click away from being eliminated.

In the world of the web, there are billions of pages of information available to the person using the web, we're just one small portion. As soon as somebody gets aggravated enough with your site, they will click off.

The reasons people get aggravated are diverse and some of them are out of our control. On the other hand, some are not out of our control.

This book will show you the most expeditious ways to create a web site to reduce the aggravation quotient, also known as the AQ, to as close to zero as possible. The anticipated result is that the visitors to your web site stay there and do what they came to do rather than clicking off and going somewhere else.

Probably the biggest offender is a trade-off called *can vs. should.* Although there are a lot of things that we can do on our web site we need to ask ourselves the question: "Should we be doing them?"

The best answer to the question is asked and answered by asking ourselves another question: "Does it help the visitor accomplish what they came to our web site for?"

The classic violation of this tenet is that we, as the authors of the site, like something so much that we put it on the web site even though it's irrelevant and distracting to the visitor. This automatically creates the AQ factor which causes people to move closer to clicking us off.

Look carefully at the things that you put on your web site. See if it's important information, or is it just animation, music, or just a lot of superfluous information that nobody really cares about except you.

Think about all the times that you had to wade through a lot of information that really was of no interest to you to get to the one or two things that were worthwhile. If your aggravation quotient reached the break over point, you would discard the book, close the magazine or the case of a web site simply click off and go somewhere else.

The visitors to your web site are no different. If their AQ hits the breaking point, they click off and they're gone.

As we stated above, one of the most critical components that is somewhat out of our control has to do with bandwidth. If you're dealing with a predominantly consumer-based marketplace, you have got to pay heed to the workarounds in this book that will help you to counter the fact that they have slow speed connections.

There are some industry wide recommendations and one of them is that your home page, when viewed with a POTS line, downloads in 10 seconds or less.

This has little or nothing to do with the rest of the web site but the problem is that many web designers make their home page (the entry page into their web site) so exotic and dazzling that it takes a long time for it to download and the visitors become frustrated enough to click off the site.

Play around with your home page a bit and notice that you can add a lot of text without significantly affecting the download time by more than a fraction of a second.

On the other hand, as soon as you start loading graphics and clip art into the page, you'll notice at the time goes up exponentially and this is what causes the AQ.

Before you jump off into the next sections, you should be aware that there are five steps in getting your web site created and available to the world:

1. Define what you want the site to do and what it should contain.

2. Outline the site.

3. Insert the content into the site's outline.

4. Establish and insert indexing and linking.

5. Publish the site.

That's it—now you're the owner of a web site!

Chapter 2 – Parts and Pieces of a Web Site

What's in a web site?

For all of the size, power, and revenues involved in the web there are only twelve components that currently make up all web sites:

1	Home page	The cover or formal entry point into the web site
2	Table of Contents	An electronic index that will help the visitor find what they're looking for—fast!
3	Site search engine	This is like asking the reference librarian to find something for you. This tool allows a visitor to type in what they are specifically looking for within the site and it will automatically take them there
4	Text	The written material in the site
5	Graphics	These include pictures, clip art, drawings, and other similar types of material
6	Sound	These include playable or downloadable files in a variety of formats like WAV and MP3
7	Video	These include playable or downloadable files in a variety of formats like AVI and MP3
8	Monitoring tools	These include simple tools like hit counters and sophisticated monitoring systems
9	Order form or shopping cart	These are systems that allow visitors to place orders for goods and services right on the site
10	BLOG	These are electronic bulletin boards where visitors can read and write messages
11	Hyperlinks	These are electronic jump points that allow the visitor to move instantaneously from one location to another with a single mouse click
12	Meta tags	These are the web site's electronic equivalent of the Dewey Decimal System that allows search engines, and the people, to locate the specific web site within the gigantic volume of the web itself

DESIGNING AN EFFECTIVE WEB SITE

As you begin to add material and elements to your web site, always keep in mind that the most successful web sites (just like books), are always written with the reader's needs and interests in mind.

Many neophytes are enamored with all the *stuff* they can do or put on a web site. Although it may be fun and appealing to you, it will probably be of little or no interest to the reader. It will simply aggravate them and provide them with a subconscious reason to click off your site and go somewhere else for the information.

As the person responsible for the ultimate outcome of the site, the actual steps in the creation of a site are as follows:

1. What is the purpose for the site?

2. How will you promote the site?

3. How will you monitor the site?

4. What content will you include in the site?

5. What measurable results can you define that will tell you whether the site is doing what it's supposed to or not?

Keep the following important points in mind when creating a site:

1. NOTHING is FREE! Make sure that you get something from the people who visit the site. Ideally, you'd like to have a credit card order, but an e-mail address, name, address, phone, or a marketing survey may as valuable to future business.

2. The web is simply a new set of tools for an old set of applications. It's mechanical—not magical. Don't expect it to do miracles for the business just because it's new and dazzling. Experience has taught that new isn't always better. The web is no exception. If current business methods are working, don't abandon them for a web site just because it's inexpensive, dazzling, and fun to play with.

3. There's a vast difference between what we can do on the web and what we should do on the web! Can means it's possible and available. Should means it helps to accomplish the primary objective in having a web site.

Anything more than that is superfluous and foolish because it detracts from the primary purpose—to do business more profitably and efficiently by using the tools of the web in lieu of some other methods. Period!

Many people believe that because color, graphics, and advertising space are relatively inexpensive on the net, that web pages should be used for everything and abandon conventional methods.

Nothing could be farther from the truth because the Internet is simply a new set of tools for an old set of applications. And just like assessing the appropriateness of conventional tools of their particular needs, we also need to assess the viability of using the tools of the Internet.

THE FOUR COMPONENTS OF WEB SITE

1. Site definition and management. This is the most important part of the process. Accurately determining what the web can do for the business and just how to structure the web site to accomplish that goal is the primary issue.

2. Site creation. This is a desktop publishing function that is known as authoring when it's applied to the web. It is comparable to graphic arts and ad copy layout. The project manager may do the work, but it's usually assigned to an experienced and competent layout and design individual.

3. Site hosting. This is the functional equivalent of paying a publication to print and run the advertising (or web site in this case). This function is called hosting and the master list of all the ISPs, some of whom are hosts, is at www.thelist.com.

4. Site maintenance. This is a combination of the three above and is a process for maintaining and updating the site so that it continues to perform effectively as a business and marketing tool.

In addition, here are several critical thoughts for consideration before embarking on a thoughtless plunge into the world of creating a web site for Internet marketing, advertising, and business:

• What is the purpose of the web page? Advertising, information, catalog, order capture, surveys, or two-step programs?

• Have you planned on notifying clients or prospects about your cyberspace presence through conventional advertising methods such as magazines, newspaper, mail, and broadcast? Clients are not psychics! The responsibility for notifying them about your cyberspace presence is up to you.

• Have you determined what percentages of your prospects are online? If they're not or are afraid of computers, the Internet is not a medium that they will use.

• Is there an advantage to the clients doing business with you online or is the Internet more trouble than it is worth?

If clients or prospects don't believe that using your web site will make them money, save them money, or save them time, they probably won't use it. If you insist on it, they may cease to do business with you.

LAYOUT AND PLANNING

For most people, the first *book* we ever wrote was a term paper and the teacher told us that the first step was to outline the material before we started the actual writing tasks.

Since a web site is an electronic book, the process is identical and experienced web designers will tell you that this step will save you countless hours of frustration by carefully planning the task before you begin.

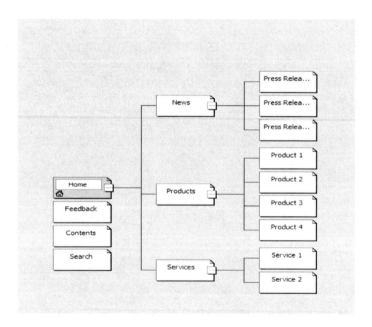
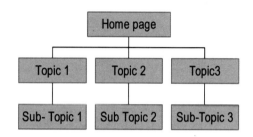

The diagram shown above on the left side is known as a *Navigation Page*. This particular one was created using Microsoft FrontPage and it's an invaluable tool during the actual development of the web site because it automatically changes as you add or delete pages.

If you prefer, you can use a manual system or any kind of block diagram software (like the one done in Word above) to create your own outline.

Whichever method you choose, by creating a printable outline and marking off the different pages as you fill in the content, you'll have a running record of what's done, what's not, and how much is left before the site is complete.

NAMING YOUR WEB SITE

The name for your web site, or electronic book, is called your domain. This is technically called a universal resource locator or URL. These domains can be obtained from a variety of sources and at a wide range of prices.

No matter who you buy your domain name from, it's always going to be registered with Network Solutions, the company that maintains the master repository of domain names throughout the world.

Network Solutions receive a small portion of the annual renewal fee for your domain. This covers their costs for maintaining the database in a worldwide configuration.

The difference between the small amount of money that Network Solutions receives for the database maintenance and the price you paid for your domain name is nothing more than a sales commission. Therefore, it's in your best interest for you to shop for the best deals on domain names.

We currently recommend www.godaddy.com and www.1and1.com as the places to research and purchase your domain names. These two companies are currently the largest suppliers and have the best prices for obtaining domain names.

RENTING SERVER SPACE

The electronic bookshelf that holds your web site is called the server and in order to make your web site available to the rest of the web world you need to rent some server space. These server spaces are nothing more than space on a hard disk drive that is set-up as a public bookshelf for your web site.

In addition to supplying domain names at the best prices, www.godaddy.com and www.1and1.com also supply server space at the best prices.

As shown in the accompanying diagrams, you can purchase a domain name with over 25 MB of space for less than five dollars a month. For about 80 percent of the web site requirements, this particular combination will be more than adequate.

If, on the other hand, you need more space or more features, your ISP will be happy to rent you what ever you need at reasonable prices.

How much server space do you need? Since server space an electronic bookshelf space, the answer depends on what you're putting on your web site.

You can put over thousand pages of text in 8 to 10 MB depending on the fonts, formatting and other factors.

This means that a 25 MB site will give you about 2500 pages of text and that's a lot of writing.

When you start putting graphics, audio and video on your site you start to require a lot of additional space.

For example a single 1½ x 1½ inch JPEG photo, either black and white or color, requires about 250 KB while and 8 x 5 color print scanned at 75 DPI and saved as a JPEG requires 175 KB. If you take a single 5 x 7 color photo scanned at 150 dots per inch and save it as a JPEG you'll need over 400 KB.

Take a realistic look at what you're going to be putting on the web site before you decide how much space to rent.

Don't forget that if you need more, you can always rent more, but most of the people who purchase a web site buy more space than they need and end up paying for something that they're not using.

PUBLISHING YOUR WEB SITE

Publishing your web site, for all practical purposes, is nothing more than copying the web site that you have created on your computer to your server space.

Depending on the software that you use the sequence might be slightly different but it basically involves the following steps:

1. Select the *publish* or *copy* to your web site feature on your software.

2. After you type in your domain and assuming that you are connected to the Internet, your software will ask you for the name and password that you have been assigned.

3. After you clear the name and password hurdle, you are now free to perform the following functions:

   • You can copy the entire web site that you created from your computer to your server space.

   • You can copy only the pages that you have changed since the last time you worked on your web site.

   • You can log directly onto your web site and make the changes on the web site without making the changes on your computer.

   • You can reverse the procedure and copy the entire web site from your server back onto the hard drive of your computer. This is done as a technique for providing a backup in the event that the server that holds your web site crashes for some unknown reason.

One more recommendation is that once you have your web site up and running, that you copy it from the server to your hard drive and then put it on a CD and store it in a safe place. This way you'll always have a hard copy in the event that something goes wrong.

Specify the location	Enter name and password	Publish

Web Site Content

A web site is a book, a billboard, an advertisement, a catalog, or a collection of documents that are stored in cyberspace and are available for anyone connected to the Internet.

Our purpose here is for you to think carefully about the purpose of the web site and what you want it to accomplish. Then you can decide if you want to be the one to actually create the web site content.

Home Page

Successful authors will tell you that no matter how well you write, you need a cover artist to design the book cover so that it's appealing to the buying public.

Web sites are a little different but the basic tenants still hold true. Here's how a web site is structured:

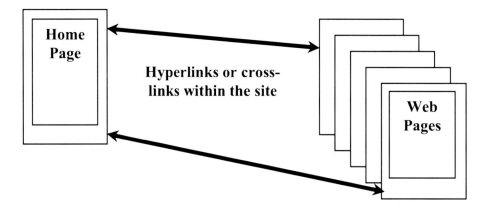

There is a basic dichotomy in designing the home page for web site.

On one hand, we are considering our web site to be an electronic book and like a book, we want to the cover to be dazzling, dramatic, and engaging.

The problem with doing this on the cover of our web page is that the more complex and graphically intense we make the home page, the longer it takes for the user to download and display it on their computer.

This may not be a problem if the user is viewing the web site with a high-speed Internet connection. On the other hand, if the user is using a POTS line, the problems are compounded because the dazzling content seems to take forever to load and the visitor's AQ rises sharply.

Successful web site developers have discovered that having a relatively simple home page containing the bare essentials is the best tradeoff. This philosophy has nothing to do with the site content and relates only to the home page so that the visitor is not immediately greeted with long download delays before being able to view the contents of this site.

This flies in the face of graphic artists who feel that the web site is a blank canvas to be filled with their dazzling graphics and overwhelming talent.

This would be OK if your web site was totally dedicated to graphic arts. However, if the site has something to do with a topic other than dazzling graphics, there is no practical reason, other than your own personal love of a graphically dynamic home page, to have that level of complexity greet a visitor.

As we'll explain below, the best things to have on the home page are:

- organizational identification (logos, etc.)

- contact information

- purpose for the site

- hyperlink table of contents

- site search engine

You may want to put color, background art, graphics and photographs on the home page but be careful to not overdo it simply because you can.

The chances are still about 40-60 that the visitor will have a slow speed connection and your graphics will aggravate them and remind them that you're really wasting their time instead of getting right to the meat of the web site.

Table of Contents

Since the web is an electronic book, think about going to a bookstore and looking for specific topic. After you find a book that you think is of interest to you, you'll probably look for the table of contents to see if what you're specifically interested in is listed. After that, you'll look at the content.

Web sites are no different and on your home page we recommend that you have a hyperlinked table of contents. One of the best examples is www.Staples.com.

You'll notice that their web site home page is not graphically dynamic, but it is very user friendly. Notice that everything is hyperlinked so if you want something specific, all you have to do is click on that particular link and it'll take you right out to that page.

SITE SEARCH ENGINE

One of the standard built-in tools on most of the high-end web site authoring software is a site search engine.

This is an easily installed component tool that allows you to place a little box, like the example we've shown in Office Depot's site, that allows the visitor to type in names, part numbers or anything that they're searching for.

Once they ask the site search engine for specifics, the site search engine will search within the boundaries of the site itself and bring back the actual location where of that search term is located.

We highly recommend putting both the hyperlinked table of contents and the site search engine on the home page to ensure that visitors can immediately locate what they're looking for, do their business, and not click off and go someplace else that's less frustrating or irritating.

Below is an example using our web site. Notice that we've simplified the table of contents into a block diagram with hypertext links and provided a site search engine.

For example, if you look on our web site for *books*, the search engine will bring back all of the places on our web site where the word books appears, and each one will be hyperlinked.

By clicking on that link, you'll go to specific points within the web site without having to search the entire web site and maybe not finding what you're looking for.

TEXT

A web site is, after all, a book, so you would expect to find text in this book.

One of the interesting things that have happened with the web since there is no practical restriction on the amount that people can write is that people tend to become overly verbose and write a lot more material on a web site than is actually needed.

The question really becomes a decision as to how much information the visitor requires to satisfy their needs. In other words, do you need to supply long copy, short copy, or bulleted text?

A significant statistic that should govern your writing is that of those that read, 80 percent are skimmers. What this means is that they usually read headlines and bullet points and generally don't go any further.

The fact is that even though you like to write long copy, the visitors to the web site won't necessarily read the long copy.

Fortunately the web allows you the opportunity to give visitors a choice, and giving people their choice will help reduce the AQ faster than anything else.

What this means to you is that you can start by writing your text in short copy (or preferably in bulleted text). Get people's attention with headlines, bullet points or a condensed amount of information.

If they need even more extensive information, they can click for the long copy and get even more information until such time as they have enough information to satisfy the requirements that they had when they entered the web site.

A wonderful example of how this works is done on www.Amazon.com.

The following slides represent a book called Clutterology, Getting Rid of Clutter and Getting Organized, by Nancy Miller.

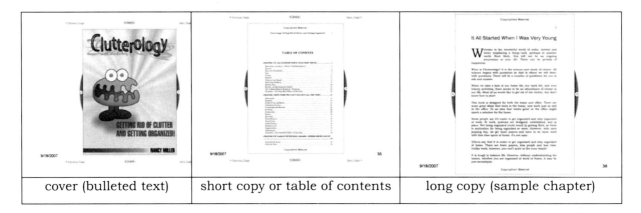

| cover (bulleted text) | short copy or table of contents | long copy (sample chapter) |

Amazon.com has provided a multi-page click system that allows you to view short, medium and long portions of the book depending on the visitor needs. Notice that the first one includes only the cover which is the functional equivalent of a headline and bullet points.

The second click takes you to the table of contents and that would be the equivalent of short copy.

The next click takes you to a sample chapter and that would be the long copy. The question is: "How much information do you need to supply the visitor so that they have what they came for?"

The next example is from one of our clients, Pamela Samuels Young. Pamela is a successful mystery writer and on her web site, she has included a sample chapter from her book, Every Reasonable Doubt.

This allows visitors to sample her writing style, which is pretty much what you do when you flip through a book at the bookstore to make a decision and buy the book.

GRAPHICS

If there was one thing that made the web extremely popular almost overnight, it was its ability to display color graphics.

When the web added in the components of color, motion and pictures, it became very user friendly and it was like looking at color television.

Graphics include a variety of things including clip art, photos, and backgrounds that can be color, black and white, or a variety of different halftones and sepia formats.

Graphics are important in making points, showing images of products and events, and separating a lot of text. Visit a site called Clipart.com (www.clipart.com). Clipart.com has over 9 million pieces of royalty-free graphics, clip art and photos, that you can use on your web site.

When you visit this site, you can use their search engine and can review and download all 9 million pieces of clip art for free. However, to prevent you from using them for free, they have a banner across the front of the picture that boldly displays the words Clipart.com.

To use the clip art without the Clipart.com banner, you have to pay approximately $18 a month or $120 a year for subscription.

Here is a specific caution about graphics: Never search the Internet for clip art and use it on your web site! There's a good possibility that it's copyrighted art and you'll be inviting a lawsuit under the federal forgery and counterfeiting laws.

Always use authorized art and graphics on your web site. Of course, if you generate them yourself, then you don't have any problems.

ANI GIFS

There is one type of graphic that is prevalent in a lot of amateur sites and virtually nonexistent on professional sites. These are known as Ana GIFs which is short for animated graphics.

You can literally get thousands of Ana GIFs for free at sites like www.virtuallandmedia.com/ani-gifs.htm and Microsoft's Design Gallery Live offers many animated GIFs as part of their offerings at http://office.microsoft.com/en-us/clipart/default.aspx.

Ana GIFs are little animated characters that tend to grab our attention because of their motion and color. Although they look clever, they're actually somewhat self-destructive to the web sites in which they are used. The reasons are:

1. They take a long time to download. If you've ever played with a flipbook that made a horse jump over a hedge by flipping the pages, the horse moved because the horse is in several different positions.

    This is how Ana GIFs create motion and require six different positions of the graphic to create an activity. In addition, you have to download and activate the software to make the six different graphics rotate through their sequence which results in seven files that have to be downloaded in order to make a ball spin, lightning flash, eyeballs move, or a book flip through its pages.

One special note is that whether the Ani GIFs is very small and located in the corner of the page or very large and takes up the bulk of the page, you still have to download the seven files.

If you put three of them on a page, that's 21 graphic files that have to be downloaded before you get the effect. This causes the aggravation quotient to rise sharply.

2. Motion and sound attract attention, and conversely, can also distract. If you have important information on your web page that you want the visitors to view and their attention is distracted by an Ani GIFs, you've actually defeated the purpose of the important parts of the web page.

Although there are literally millions of free Ani GIFs available that you can put on a web site, we really don't recommend that you use them unless there is some especially outstanding point on a page that you just don't want people to overlook.

PHOTOS

Photos are wonderful and an integral part of the web as we know it today. They're important because they add realism color and clarity. But don't forget photos take time to download.

The photo that you see here is of the author at the Hollywood Christmas Parade. This is a great photo [especially in color] but the file is 15 MB in size and takes a long time to download if the viewer has a POTS line.

One of the best techniques for getting around sending big photo files is to use a process called thumbnailing. The process is rather simple and straightforward. It is included in the better software development packages.

The process is relatively simple and straightforward:

1. Insert the photo that you want to add to the web site to your web page.

2. Click on the photo.

3. From the menu of commands, select thumbnail and click it.

You'll notice that the large photograph has now been converted to a postage stamp sized photo called a thumbnail. This photo has highly reduced resolution content.

When a visitor to the web site sees the thumbnail, they get a relative idea of the photo but not a clear picture. By simply putting their mouse on the thumbnail and double-clicking, the small picture will go away and the large picture will download although it may take a fairly long time.

This thumbnailing technique is used to supply visitors with a lot of rough information from which they can select a high-resolution picture by simply clicking on the thumbnail.

The two photos below are perfect examples of how this works. Here is a photograph from our web site.

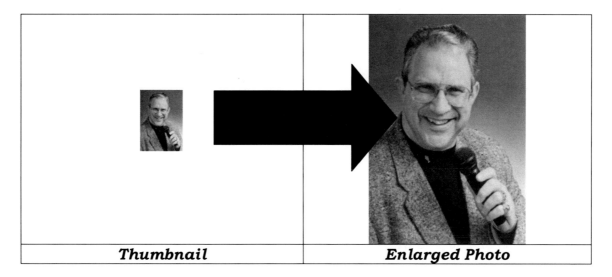

Thumbnail	*Enlarged Photo*

By clicking on the small picture, the large picture appears giving you all the details that you need.

This is a common technique and highly recommended for getting a lot of information of a graphic nature downloaded on the visitor's computer without raising the AQ.

Formats

There are currently about 150 different formats that you can use to capture, store, view, and edit pictures. However, the web pretty much dictates that we use two primary formats, GIFs and JPEGs. Whenever possible convert everything on your web site to a JPEG because it is a good clear format and has a small file size.

Can You See The Difference?	
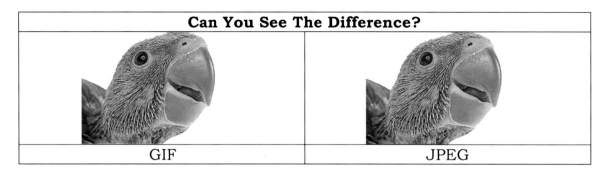	
GIF	JPEG

For example, a JPEG of 2000 bytes of information converted to a GIF will be about 6000 bytes of information. This means that the GIF, although technically superior in quality to the JPEG, will take three times as much storage space and three times as long to download.

All of the high-end web authoring software comes with converters. If you don't have this kind of converter on your software you can go to a site called www.spinwave.com and use their conversion tool called the cruncher. The cruncher allows you to put JPEGs in and they come out as GIFs. Or GIFs in and JPEGs out.

Because of the viewing limitations of the web and the display hardware connected with it, it's doubtful that using GIF formatted graphics will look any better to the visitor, so always use JPEGs if at all possible.

Sources

One of the most popular places to get pictures these days is to take your film to your local processing facility and ask for them back on CD-ROM. Once you have the files on CD-ROM, you can view them on your computer and cut and paste them into your web site.

You can also use your 35mm camera and a scanner, which is the way we originally inputted photos before the days of digital cameras.

When you take photographs with your camera and use a scanner to convert them to digital format, make sure that you set the scan resolution at the lowest resolution which is generally 70 to 72 DPI (Dots Per Inch).

The reason is that the web does not generally reproduce any graphics higher than 72 dots per inch because most of the viewing components, like the monitor, don't support it.

You can also buy collections of photos on CD and there are a variety of resources like www.clipart.com that can supply them for you.

The last, and most prevalent way that we're getting stuff onto our web sites these days, is with a digital camera and since digital cameras have become so inexpensive and readily available, this is what you'll probably be using.

In order to understand what you're dealing with a digital camera, take a look at pixels.

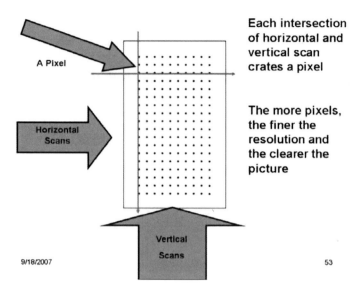

A Pixel

Horizontal Scans

Vertical Scans

9/18/2007

53

Each intersection of horizontal and vertical scan crates a pixel

The more pixels, the finer the resolution and the clearer the picture

In today's market-driven economy, more and more promotion is going into higher and higher mega pixel cameras. What this means is that for every inch of the image there are more dots and the more dots you have per inch, the finer the resolution and the greater the detail.

The problem that we have with the web is that above 72 dots per inch or about a 1.2-mega-pixel camera, you cannot differentiate the difference.

The reason for this, contrary to all of the marketing hype and promotion, is that although you can supply a high-resolution, high-definition photo, the system called the web along with the monitors and display systems can't usually display them in the higher resolution format.

In fact very few people who have high-mega pixel cameras have ever actually seen the improved resolution that you get from going from a 2-mega-pixel camera to a 10-mega-pixel camera, except for the cost in their wallet.

Everything that you need to put photos on the web site can be done for

about $100. All you need is a four mega pixel camera with a three times optical zoom lens and an LCD display.

These can be found on the web for anywhere from $40-$99.

There is another problem with putting extremely high-resolution pictures on the web site and the best example we can give you is with our client Pamela Samuels Young.

On her web site for her book, Every

Reasonable Doubt, she has a series of high-resolution photos including a cover of her book. This high-resolution picture is not there so you can view it in high-resolution but so that a bookstore, who is hosting a signing, can download it, put it on a CD-ROM, and take it to FedEx Kinko's and have it blown up into a poster.

The high-resolution picture is made available so that when they expand or blow it up, that the picture remains clear and doesn't get grainy.

When you try and look at the same high-resolution picture on a relatively low-resolution viewing system, such as your monitor, you end up with what's called a *porthole effect* where you only get to see is part of the picture at a time.

The reason is that the total number of dots or pixels that make up the picture are greater than your monitor can reproduce at one time. It only displays as many pixels as it has the capability of and the rest of them are either off to the side or below the screen.

SOUND

The Internet, like all computer programs, started out as a text-based system with a bunch of beeps and dings as indicators for commands and other signaling functions.

Along with an enhanced graphics capability, the web provides the ability to supply digital quality sound in a variety of formats for the visitor to hear.

The current trend is to supply music in the MP3 format in the form of subscription programs such as iTunes and the newly reorganized Napster. These sites allow you to pay a fixed price to download music on your computer, MP3 or iPod.

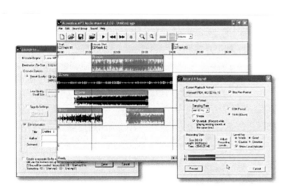

You can supply audio material on your web site by first creating it and editing it with digital software. Most new computers come with all of the software that you need to record and edit sound but if you need a recommendation, look at www.acoustica.com. They have a $25 recording and editing software package called Acoustica MP3 Audio Mixer that will allow you to work on 64 tracks simultaneously.

When you have the sounds edited the way you want them, you'll need to save them and then copy them to the web site.

MP3 is the preferred method of storage because it's a compressed technique that takes less space to store and less time to download. On the other hand, if you think people are going to need the conventional wave format, save and store your audio material as wave files. Either way, your authoring software will allow you to store the file on the web site and provide a link to activate and play it.

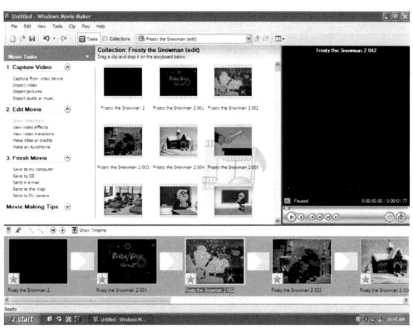

With improvements in web development software, and the web's software tools themselves, virtually everything, including music and video, is treated as an object or a file that can be accessed by the visitor by simply clicking on it with their mouse.

VIDEO

Depending on what you're using your site for, you may want to supply the visitor with either sample video clips or complete video performances, such as commercials for products and services, or recorded events.

As mentioned above in the sound section, video is now treated as a file, just as though it were a graphic or photograph. The software for playing videos is now standard on virtually all computers so as a web site designer, all you have to do is supply the content and the user's systems will automatically play.

There are a variety of new technologies available for creating video content including digital videotape, DVDs, video cameras with a hard disk drive and cable to transfer the recorded material directly to the PC plus video cameras that record their content directly to memory cards or flash drives that can be inserted into the computer for editing.

Many of the latest digital cameras have the capability of recording sound and video, as well as single pictures, on their memory card.

These files can be in AVI, MP3, MP4, or whatever format is the most usable for the visitor.

Once recorded, the information can be transferred to a computer and edited with either the included software packages such as the Windows Movie Maker or with other video editing packages.

RCA "Small Wonder"

30 minutes of video

$99

Supacam

60 minutes of video

$99

One of the latest stand-alone innovations for generating video is RCA's Small Wonder camera. For less than $100 you can have a video equivalent of a point and shoot film camera that will record up to 30 minutes on internal memory systems. Once recorded, the material is copied to your computer, edited, and stored on a web site for clicking and downloading by the visitor.

The only caution in using video is the about the visitors download speed capabilities. Video files are some of the largest on the Internet. Although the web streams the video (pre-loads part of the video while you're still looking at some of the video and continues to download faster than you can view), viewing video on a POTS line tends to be aggravating.

Most of the software now allows the visitor, even with a POTS line, to download the video content to their computer's hard drive, taking as much time as necessary to complete the task.

Once downloaded, the visitor can play it at full speed with their media player.

MONITORING SOFTWARE

Monitoring software, although inherently viable, has become more of a nuisance and a time waster to most web site developers than about anything else.

This Many People Have Been to MY Page:

0123456789

The most basic form of web site monitoring software is known as a hits counter. These are software additions; usually a tool included with the software development package. That allows you to see how many people have visited a web site or a specific page. They count up like an odometer on a car.

Several years ago an advertising executive said that HITS is an acronym that stands for *how idiots track sales.*

His logic was that knowing the number of hits or unspecified visitors you get on a web site is basically irrelevant because you don't know anything about the visitors, what they were really interested in, where they came from, or what they would really like to do once they're on your web site. Subsequently, most professional web sites took the hit counters off of their web sites.

SuperStats Standard provides detailed reports on the number of visitors to your site as well as search engines and keywords that are driving visitors to your site.

SuperStats Professional provides reports that include visitor analysis, marketing reports, search engine tracking, and details on the pages visited from entry to exit.

SuperStats Premium gives you hundreds of reports including unique tools to support e-commerce web site tracking, detailed HTML analysis, and site performance tools.

If you're really serious about monitoring the performance of your web site, do a web search for *web site monitoring software* and you'll get a variety of choices including software like www.webstats.com.

Webstats.com is one of the most comprehensive and detailed monitoring systems available on the Internet and although it's a little pricey, it'll tell you more about what's going on with your web site and its visitors.

These packages of information, which are available as an automatic e-mail memo to you or as an online viewable report once you enter your name and password, cost from $10 to $30 per month and can include the following information about your site:

- Advertising and commerce reports to track the ROI (return on investment) of your campaigns.

- Click fraud detection.

- Click paths, geography, and technology reports.

- Detailed visitor navigation reports with unique click path analysis feature.

- Detailed web site analysis and visitor behavior reports.

- Different web site traffic reports.

- Organic and paid search engine reports.

- Referral reports.

- Search engine traffic and search phrase reports.

- Standard and specific time periods.

- Tracks page views, visits and unique visitors.

For as wonderful as these statistics sound, the primary question becomes: "What are you going to do with them once you have them?"

From a project management standpoint, web site monitoring software makes an excellent tool for finding out if the web site, and everything connected with its operation, is functioning properly.

This means that in order to make the monitoring software useful, the form, function and objectives of the web site must be clearly and precisely defined so that you can review the statistics obtained from web stats against the projected success of the web site itself.

The discrepancies between the planned operation of the web site and the actual results obtained can then be used to initiate changes to the web site to help ensure that it functions as planned.

For a simplistic as this sounds, it's actually a major business decision and requires a full time person to compare the marketing aspects of the web site against the actual results obtained from the monitoring software into a conscientious analysis of what's right, what's wrong, and what needs to be done in order to bring the site into compliance with the marketing plans.

The bottom line is that if you are planning on creating a detailed project plan where your web site becomes an integral part of that plan and its success will be monitored and modified accordingly, then monitoring software is probably a cheap investment to help ensure your success.

If, on the other hand, you're primarily interested in getting the material up on the web site even if it has flaws, then the monitoring software will be a waste of time and money because it will only serve to remind you that there are inequities in the site and you still haven't fixed them.

ORDER FORM (SHOPPING CART)

Shopping cart software is specialized software used in e-commerce to assist people making purchases online, analogous to the term shopping cart.

The software allows online customers to place items in the cart. When they checkout, the software typically calculates a total including shipping charges and taxes, as applicable.

These software applications typically provide a means of capturing a client's payment information, and although the simplest shopping carts strictly allow for an item to be added to a basket to start a checkout process (for example the free PayPal shopping cart), most shopping cart software actually provides additional features that an Internet merchant uses to fully manage an online store.

Shopping cart software typically consists of two components:

Storefront: the area of the web store that is accessed by visitors to online shop. Category, product, and other pages (for example search, best sellers, etc.) are dynamically generated by the software based on the information saved in the store database.

Administration: the area of the web store that is accessed by the merchant to manage the online shop. The number of administrative features changes depending on the sophistication of the shopping cart software. In general, a store manager is able to add and edit products, categories, discounts, shipping and payment settings, etc. Order administration features are also included in many shopping cart programs.

Before we jump into the specifics of the shopping cart itself, we need to look at your objective in offering something to the visitor from your site: Are you interested in instant sales or list generation?

In the world of marketing there are two primary philosophies:

1. Get somebody to place an order now and

2. Generate a targeted mailing list so that future sales can be made as a result of the list.

The web has become somewhat deceptive in its ability to accurately capture targeted mailing lists although there are some proven techniques that will help you to achieve this goal.

Let's look at two examples of how the web is very effective in the marketing world. The first is what is known as a coupon site this is a site that people visit in order to obtain free grocery coupons in their vicinity.

The process is relatively straightforward: When you visit the site, you are required to submit your ZIP code and fill out what is generically known as a guestbook. This may include name, address, city, state, ZIP, e-mail, and perhaps the answers to some questions.

Once you have filled out the guestbook and answered these questions you can have access to the your choice of free coupons noting that they

had been specifically targeted to your geographic area.

Once you have selected the coupons, you can simply download and print them out so they can be taken to the store and be redeemed.

Compare that to the site call Stacks. This is a catalog site and since statistically, people still like to read paper catalogs, Stacks has made it very easy for you to obtain over 200 catalogs by simply going through and selecting them with your mouse.

Like the coupon site, you must enter a ZIP code and fill out a guestbook prior to having the catalogs mailed to you.

Now here's a comparison between the two sites:

1. On the coupon site, notice that the attraction to the site is free coupons, the price that you pay for the coupons (remember, nothing is free on the net), is TDI or targeted demographic information. Also notice that the delivery vehicle is the web itself so there are no additional costs or efforts for printing, postage or handling.

2. On the Stacks site the attraction is the free catalogs, the payment is your TDI, but this time we have conventional postage, printing and handling in order to get the material to the visitors.

The difference between the two sites is that on the coupon site, the visitor does not have to enter accurate demographic information in order to receive the coupons. If the address data entered is flawed you'll end up with a lot of Nixies or undeliverable addresses in your database.

As you create your web site and especially, your customer service and shopping areas, look carefully at what you ultimately want to achieve before you decide on an all-electronic system that may leave you with a lot of flawed database information.

Let's move on to the software to capture the visitor's ordering information.

Shopping cart software can be generally categorized into two categories:

1. Licensed software: The software is downloaded and then installed on your web server. This is most often associated with a one-time fee, although there are many free products available as well.

Look into Shop Factory (www.shopfactory.com). This is a comprehensive shopping cart program for about $300. You can download and test the entire package from their web site for free. You can test it on your computer but you just can't publish it to your web site until you pay for it.

The main advantage of this option is that you own a license and can host it on any web server that meets the server requirements, and that the source code can often be accessed and edited to customize the application.

The other element is that in order to accept credit cards from shoppers on your web site, you'll need to establish a merchant account that allows your business to accept credit cards, debit cards, gift cards and other forms of payment cards. This is also widely known as payment processing or credit card processing.

Business owners who receive credit card payment for their goods or services, must apply for a merchant account typically through a merchant bank or MSP (Merchant Service Provider). The merchant account will typically be established based on several factors.

Merchant accounts are not free—a variety of charges are involved. Some fees are charged on a monthly basis but most are charged on a per-item or percentage basis.

The monthly fees are at the discretion of the merchant account provider but the majority of the per-item and percentage fees are passed through the merchant account provider to the issuing bank according to a schedule of rates called Interchange fees, which are set by Visa and MasterCard.

2. Shopping Cart Services: these are services like PayPal who provide everything you'll need to install a comprehensive shopping cart on your web site including the ability to process the client's credit card order complete with tax, shipping, and a variety of other calculations if needed.

The big advantage of PayPal is that you're simply *brokering* the business and they actually handle the transaction for you.

This means you don't have to undergo financial vetting and since it's technically their processing efforts, it's free and they don't charge any fees or percentages except when a transaction is actually made. At this point, you can plan on them keeping about 5-6 percent of the total transaction for their services.

PAY PER DOWNLOAD SERVICE

For as long as the web has been around, there has been a process called pay per download that allows the visitor to enter their credit card and download software, audio, video, and any form of electronically deliverable material.

Recently a new service called Payloadz has been developed by PayPal that provides this once very expensive service to virtually anybody who wants to use it. It's called Payloadz and it's available from www.Payloadz.com.

The philosophy is quite simple:

1. You register with Payloadz.

2. You fill out their electronic shopping cart.

3. You upload the material to be sold via download.

Payloadz provides a link to the pay per download site so that you can put it on your web page. When the visitor wants to buy a downloadable item, such as audio, video, software, or a database, they simply click on the button and they will be linked to the payload site.

Once there, they will be required to enter their credit card information and once it's approved, they can download the material directly to their computer.

This is the same kind of system that iTunes and other related MP3 music systems have capitalized on so extensively in the last couple of years.

The payload system has several different options including what's known as their *Premium Merchant Account* which is free until somebody pays for download.

At that time, they deduct a 15 percent handling fee and although this may seem a little expensive, unlike printing paper materials, you have absolutely no additional cost and that of the sales price is available to you immediately from virtually doing nothing.

BLOGS

Before we explain what BLOGS and how they are used, we need to review where the word BLOG came from.

The original term was web log. If you try and say it fast, you may find it difficult, and that's what a news reporter did one day and slurred the two words into the word BLOG.

From then on, it became known as the BLOG.

So what is a BLOG? For all practical purposes, it's an electronic scratch pad on your web site that allows people, including yourself, to leave messages.

If this seems overly simplistic in light of what's going on in the world today with BLOGS, just stop and think about. They are simply a place to send and receive messages about a particular topic that is usually associated with the web site that hosts the BLOG.

As a general rule, BLOGS are free for anyone who owns a web site. The example shown here is from our web site host, www.1and1.com, and they provide us with a free BLOG that can be configured to meet our needs.

You can find all kinds of free BLOGS on the web by simply typing in the words free BLOGS to a search tool such as Google or Yahoo!. Once you arrive at the BLOG set-up side, the instructions will show you how to walk yourself through it and add it to your web site.

My "Clueless" Blog - FREE from my ISP

Most BLOGS give you the choice of being supervised or unsupervised. The difference between them is as follows:

1. Unsupervised BLOGS: With an unsupervised BLOG, as soon as the visitor leaves a message and presses the enter key, the message is immediately posted to the BLOG's bulletin board. Anyone in the world who logs on to the BLOG can immediately see and respond to it.

2. Supervised BLOGs: Supervised BLOGs actually allow someone to monitor or censor what is left on the BLOG and then decide whether or not it will be allow to be posted on the BLOG for everyone to see and comment on.

BLOGs are highly controversial since they become a form for people's ranting, raving, and in many cases overzealous opinions.

The original form of the BLOG was called a USENET newsgroup and in the early days of the Internet, these USENET groups were responsible for the explosive growth of the Internet so the power and importance of BLOGs is not to be dismissed.

The problem with BLOGs is that since there is no set of guidelines, rules, regulations, or laws governing what goes on in them and the information left on them is highly controversial and subject to interpretation by the people who read.

There are two pertinent points about putting up a BLOG that you want to be careful:

1. The copyright issue—if you are planning on using, reprinting, and/or publishing the information that people leave on your BLOG, be sure to include a statement that says that whatever they leave their now belongs to you and they cannot claim copyright or demand royalties or any kind of recognition. There are many people who are currently using the information left on BLOGs as basic research information.

2. Make sure you recognize and acknowledge that anything posted and displayed on a BLOG is simply an opinion and is not verified as being factual. This can become important if people are looking to your BLOG for something significant where they're going to use the information to make a decision.

Since this is a part of your web site where you are not actually creating the content, you need to be aware of the potential liabilities and hazards of freely allowing others to leave *stuff* on your site.

There are a variety of legal disclaimers that you can get and to make sure that you're not held responsible for what somebody else leaves on your BLOG, we strongly recommend that you include these disclaimers on your site.

A BLOG disclaimer can say anything, but here are some things that you may consider if you are putting together your own disclaimer.

Content Validity: A BLOG is always in transition. The information you publish today might not be valid or accurate two weeks or two years from now. Content, sources, information and links change over time, so make sure you protect yourself from the natural evolution of BLOG content.

Content Accuracy: We all make mistakes. The disclaimer should take the accuracy and validity of your BLOG's content into account.

External Links: What you link to reflects back on your BLOG. URLs and domains change hands. Protect yourself in your BLOG's disclaimer from what is at the end of a link, as well as from those linking to you.

Photographs and Graphic Images: If you are using images that are not yours, then say so. If they yours, make sure you claim them and hold yourself harmless from any harm caused by the images, such as offending someone.

Files, Programs, and Downloadables: If you offer downloadable files or programs, such as WordPress Plug-Ins, Themes, etc., make sure you get the wording exactly right to protect yourself in case your file damages or harms someone's BLOG, site, or computer.

Libel and Defame: Be clear that anyone reading your BLOG will not hold you libel for what you say or display. State the content on the BLOG is the opinion of the BLOGger, not intended to "malign any religion, ethnic group, club, organization, company, or individual," or anyone or thing, especially those with the ability and desire to fight back.

Responsibility: You should state that you are responsible for the content, not your employer, volunteer group, membership organization, church, or other agencies which you might be seen to represent. Take care with this. If you volunteer for an organization, and BLOG about it, you could be seen to *represent* it through implication, just as much as you might be representing your employer if you write about the company and/or your work.

Personal Views: State that these are your personal views, which implies you are responsible for them, not your employee or another agency. Your BLOG is your opinion.

Protection from Commenters: Consider stating that you are not responsible, nor will be held liable, for anything anyone says on your BLOG in the BLOG comments, nor the laws which they may break in your country or theirs through their comments' content, implication, and intent.

Protection from Fellow BLOGgers: If you have multiple BLOGgers and/or contributors on your BLOG, consider some statement that covers them, protecting them but also protecting you from what they say in their BLOG posts.

Do No Harm: It helps when you say that your *intention* is to do no harm. To not injure others, defame, or libel, just in case someone thinks you are doing harm. *Harm* is subject to interpretation not facts. It's your opinion and advice, not counsel. What you write on your BLOG is not to be taken as fact nor absolute. If people use your advice, tips, techniques, and recommendations, and are injured, you are not to be held responsible.

Disclosure of Paid-to-BLOG: Some disclaimers may include a disclosure statement that says the BLOG's content is, or is not, generated to make money or paid for BLOGging content. If this is not included in the disclaimer, make sure you publicly and visibly post a disclosure, as there is a growing call for BLOGger's honesty.

Language Issues: Language is a tricky thing, so consider adding a statement about not being responsible for translation or interpretation of content. Also, if this issue is important to you, you know that punctuation can change the intent of a statement, so hold yourself and your BLOG harmless from prosecution for bad grammar and punctuation.

Copyright: If you want to make your disclaimer a catchall, be sure to include a statement on your copyright policy, setting the guidelines for how and when your content may be used by others.

International and Cultural Laws: If your BLOG is read by someone from another country, a country which has laws which restricts or censors content, and your BLOG's content crosses their line, who is responsible for *crossing the border*? Is it you or the reader? Either way, consider a statement that says you are not responsible for defamatory statements bound to government, religious, or other laws from the reader's country of origin.

Limits on Damages: Consider adding a statement restricting the financial claim that could be taken against you and your BLOG. If legal action is brought against your BLOG, it could be brought against you personally, your home, properties, and more. By setting a cap limit on the financial responsibility, it could help set a lower rate if you lose, since you publicly stated the limits.

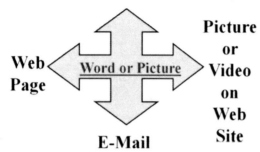

Make it Readable: Make your disclaimer readable. While legaleeze is fine, make your disclaimer easy to read and understand in plain and simple language.

Have Fun But Make it Legal: Have what fun you will with your BLOG disclaimer, making it match your BLOGging and writing style, but make sure the words are still *legal* and will protect as much as amuse your readers.

My disclaimer is that I'm not a lawyer, just giving you tips and advice, so if you want a serious disclaimer with teeth in it, have it reviewed by a lawyer to ensure it soundly protects you and your BLOG.

HYPERLINKS

Hyperlinks are the true power tool of the web. These are electronic jump points that allow the visitor to move instantaneously from one location to another with a single mouse click.

As the diagram shows, a hyperlink can instantly propel the site's visitor to:

1. Another location anywhere within the web site

2. A picture, video, graphic, or other file stored within the web site

3. Another web page anywhere on the Internet or

4. Activate the visitor's e-mail software with the site's e-mail pre-programmed so the visitor can communicate with the site's host.

The ability to hyperlink makes the web site truly transparent to the visitor.

Unlike a conventional book where page two MUST follow page one in a defined physical configuration, web pages can be located anywhere on either the user's computer or any computer on the web as long as the hyperlinks are properly configured and operational.

Hyperlink Formats

There are a number of ways to format and present hyperlinks in your web pages. What distinguishes the various formats of links are the various ways in which links are accessed. Most links are accessed via selecting (pointing and clicking) hypertext or a graphical user interface element such as a button.

Embedded link: An embedded link is a link embedded in an object such as hypertext or a hot area (the part of the page that has been designated a hyperlink).

Hot area: A hot area (image map in HTML) is an invisible area of the screen that covers a text label or graphical image.

Inline link: An inline link displays remote content without the need for embedding the content. The remote content may be accessed with or without the user selecting the link. Inline links may display specific parts of the content (for example thumbnail, low-resolution preview, cropped sections, magnified sections, description text, etc.) and access other parts or the full content when needed, as is the case with print publishing software. This allows for smaller file sizes and quicker response to changes when the full linked content is not needed, as is the case when rearranging a page layout.

Random accessed: Random-accessed linking data are links retrieved from a database or variable containers in a program when the retrieval function is from user interaction (for example dynamic menu from an address book) or non-interactive (random, calculated) process.

Hardware accessed: A hardware-accessed link is a link that activates directly via an input device (keyboard, microphone, and remote control) without the need or use of a graphical user interface.

Chapter 3 – Promoting and Linking

Now that you've completed your web site, you are part of the multibillion page electronic library known as the World Wide Web and are now faced with the same problem as everybody else who has a web site up and running: How are people going to find you?

For all the hype and rhetoric that has been put forth about being found by search engines, buying search words, and all the magic tricks for getting to the top of the search engines, the very best procedure for having your web site found is to get maximum exposure for your site.

Simply stated this means that you are better off using conventional advertising that your clients or prospects are currently experiencing and responding to for notifying them that you have a web site.

If you question the validity of this process think about every place where you see URLs listed. These include places like:

- The ends of television programs

- Announcements on radio

- Magazine advertisements

- Billboards

- Bus benches

- Buses

- And people's rear bumpers.

For as important as search engines are, the statistics tell us that most people have never been properly trained in the use of search engines. Consequently when they're looking for you, they're likely to find somebody else.

If that seems counterproductive to all the work that you've done, it probably is. So the answer to it is to make sure that your prospects or visitors to your web site type in your URL instead of a generic list of responses from a search engine.

The first step, once you have your web site up and running, is to obtain a box of splash balls from your local instant printer.

These are nothing more than peel and stick labels that look like a splash of golden paint and contain your new web address and being in color, sticking them on black-and-white correspondence will make them stand out and let people know that your web site is up and available.

As an alternative, you can use your color printer and print Avery labels and stick them on everything that you have.

Once you have established your web site, make sure that every time you change your letterheads, business cards, or any other advertising material, that you include the web address so the people will know exactly where to find your web site.

This whole concept of initially promoting and driving people back to your web site is part of a time honored and proven method of advertising called the two-step process.

The two-step process relies on small initial advertising to pique people's curiosity while simultaneously referring them to a method for obtaining additional information that will lead them to make the buying decision, whatever that turns out to be.

The example shown is from Popular Mechanics magazine, a 137-year-old publication. The ads are small space ads that appear in the back of the magazine and lack all of the power and glory necessary to get people to make a purchase.

They do however, contain enough information and graphics to get people's curiosity aroused enough to request additional information.

Traditionally an ad like the one on the left for micro-wireless cameras would have referred people to a mailing address to request a paper catalog. Notice that neither the phone number nor the snail mail address appears but instead contains the URL which will allow people to instantly go to the camera's web site and view the catalog with all of its details and pictures including the ability to make a purchase.

The operative statement here is: "New tools, old rules."

Simply stated, we are better served by advertising our web sites in places where we are reasonably sure that our prospects are going to see the advertisement rather than dropping the URL into a massive bucket of millions of URLs in a search engine and hoping that the prospects fishes us out.

Probably one of the most extreme examples of this is being done by Ask Jeeves (now www.Ask.com), and Jell-O. These organizations have made arrangements to put labels on the sides of bananas thereby creating a banana-gram with an ad that notifies people that they are available on the web.

Ask Jeeves Goes Bananas

Ask Jeeves uses a real bananna-gram to tell people where to go

Are dot-com ads taking over the world? Ask Jeeves.

The search engine recently upped the ad ante with stickers on 100 million bananas nationwide. Instead of peeling Chiquita or Dole labels off produce, consumers are confronted with Jeevsian consultations on a variety of affaires bananes.

"We wanted to place an ad where it's really relevant to people," spokeswoman

For as ludicrous as this may appear, the process is actually quite effective. Another example that we have observed is www.e-diets.com utilizing the billboard space that's built into supermarket shopping carts to advertise their weight control programs.

ONLINE DIRECTORIES

Another excellent and somewhat overlooked place to promote your web site is online telephone directories.

There are a variety of them shown in the box on the right and you'll notice that these are the electronic equivalent of Yellow Pages.

> Online Directory Sites
> www.bigfoot.com
> www.infospace.com
> www.switchboard.com
> www.whowhere.com
> www.bigbook.com

Most of them are free for users and are actually paid for by the advertisers who put billboards along the directory sites.

Unlike paper Yellow Pages, which cost hundreds perhaps even thousands of dollars to advertise in them, these sites are free and offer you an additional opportunity to gain exposure.

The logic behind using these directories is that we are never sure where the potential visitor/client is going to look for us. Since these listings are free, why not take advantage of them?

Why the Search Words are Important

When the web was originally developed and implemented, one of the initial concerns was how users of the web were going to be able to find the content that they wanted.

Since the web is the electronic equivalent of a huge library, the original developers looked to the time-honored Dewey Decimal System as a technique for indexing and finding content on the web. Unfortunately, the Dewey Decimal System doesn't work for the system that we know as the web so the developers look for alternative.

After considerable deliberation they concluded that there was no simple way to search the vast array of content although the titles of the web sites could be done relatively easily using a process similar to the Dewey Decimal System.

As a trade-off, the developers decided that the first thing that any search tool or search engine would look at would be a series of key words that the web site developers would apply to their site that would describe the overall purpose and content of the site.

These words are technically known as meta tags, although they are often referred to as keywords, index words, link words, and profile words.

Before we proceed further, it's important to note that although the search engines look at the meta tags first, each of the search engines has their own proprietary techniques (which are constantly being changed and updated) to search, link, list, and index every web site on the web.

If you are seriously concerned about how the search engines actually go about the in-depth search process, check out www.searchenginewatch.com, the premier site on the Internet that explains how each engine is currently searching and indexing web sites.

As you read this detailed report, you'll notice that it changes from month to month and each site has their own proprietary process for determining what they think is the most important content or listing element to get the searcher's information back in a hierarchical index.

There is a long and sordid history involved with getting on top of the search engines.

When the dotcom bubble burst in Y2K, the search engine's had to re-examine and redefine how they were going to allow web site developers to list and link with their sights.

Prior to the dotcom crash which redefined the economics of the Internet, you could purchase software that would allow you to change, modify, alter, and resubmit your meta tags and descriptions as often as you wanted at no charge.

The logic behind these rapid changes were spurred on by the theory that if you selected meta tags, monitored your web site, and discovered that you weren't getting the hits you wanted or weren't being listed high enough up on the search engine lists, that the fastest way to remedy this was to change the indexing words so that the next time somebody performs a search you would end up higher on the list.

The problem with this logic was, and is, that it requires an inordinate amount of time to analyze and make changes on the web site. Couple this with the technical support that was constantly being requested and

the complaints that were being received by the search engines by people who have decided that they should be listed higher than they actually were, the search engines decided to abandon the *no charge* process in favor of an optional free or fee system.

The basic system that most of the major search engines currently follow is that if you want to have control over how fast you are indexed by the engine and how you are actually listed; there is fee for each time you make a change or a modification.

Most of the major search engines charge between $200 and $300 each time you make a change which means that if you are constantly monitoring and modifying your site, it could be a very expensive proposition.

Today most web developers simply select and install meta tags on their web sites, publish them, and let the search engines perform a process called auto spidering. This auto spidering or auto indexing by the search engines is a free service that puts your web site and its meta tags into the search engine's database.

The down side to the free listing services is that indexing or re-indexing of your site, along with the way that you are listed in the search engines database, is strictly a function of the search engine and you have no control over the process. The reality is that most people really don't benefit from constantly re-indexing their web site so the bulk of all the web sites available have probably been auto spidered.

SELECTING META TAGS

The first thing that we look at when we travel through the stacks on the library is the Dewey decimal number on the spine of a book. Search engines begin their search by looking at the meta tags that have been placed on the web site. After that, depending on the algorithms and the process that the search engine has chosen to use, other elements of the web site are considered and then placed on the retrieved list.

For purposes of example in selecting meta tags, let's assume that we own a company that is in the business of toilet repair.

Logic dictates that for our meta tags we should use the words toilet, repair, and the two words as a phrase toilet and repair to cover all the possible combinations.

---

toilet

Synonyms bath, bathroom, latrine, lavatory, rest room, washroom, water closet
Related Words commode, outhouse, privy

This logic works until somebody decides to type in a word like plumbing or some word other than toilet to describe a toilet.

The inequity occurs when somebody types a word into the search engine that does not match the meta tags on our web site, our site does not match the search and we don't end up on the retrieval list.

One of the fastest and simplest ways to help ensure that you're found in the meta tag search is to use Merriam-Webster's web site (www.M-W.com) and invoke the use of their free electronic thesaurus.

Simply type in the words you have selected and let that thesaurus pick all of the common synonyms that are in use today. Once you have the synonyms, simply cut and paste them into your meta tags string.

Meta Tag Selection Tips

1. Customer surveys are best—how we would describe our web site and the words that we'd use to find our site are not necessarily the same as the visitors. If you can ask friends, relations, and clients what words they would use, you'll have a much broader array than the ones you select.

2. Include abbreviations and initials—there are a great many abbreviations and initials that we use on a daily basis instead of actually saying or writing the formal name of the organization. If there are initials or acronyms that are used to describe your organization or any of the products or services that you offer, be sure to include them in the meta tags.

3. Firm name—even though the name of your organization or firm will appear on the web site itself, the first search conducted by the search engine is on the meta tags and having your organization's name listed there will help ensure that you end up on the retrieval list.

4. Foreign words—the web is worldwide and is used by people who speak different languages. If you believe that your web site, and the material contained in it, is of interest to others who speak a language other than English, it would probably be in your best interest if you were to provide the meta tags in their multiple languages.

In order to do this all you have to do is go to www.google.com and click on their language tools.

Google offers a free service of translating words, phrases, and entire web pages from one of the language to any other language covering a variety of possibilities that will help you to make sure that you get found by people who are looking in another language.

We have included an example of a web site that is primarily in English, Bilingual Solutions International, and another example of what it looks like after it has been translated into Spanish by Google.

Google also offers complete web page translation so if the person searching for you find your content and does not speak English, they can simply type the URL into the web page translation service of a good web site and have it translated into whatever language they prefer. Conversely, if during your search you find a web site that is not in English, you can have it converted to English.

It has been noted by several linguists that the translation service provided by Google is not grammatically perfect. However, the translation is rapid and 80 to 90 percent effective so that all that is required to make a grammatically correct its final editing.

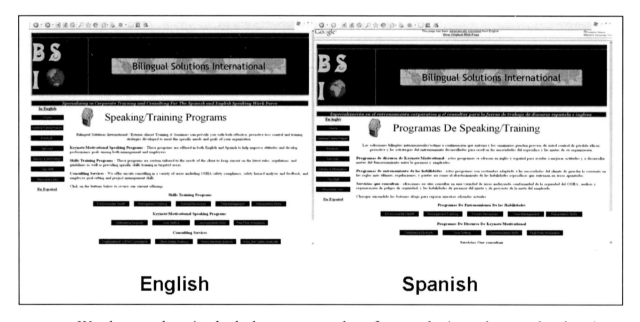

English   **Spanish**

We have also included an example of translating the author's site from English into Spanish for an immediate reference.

5. Common misspellings—One of the cleverest things that you can do is to take the most common meta tags used to describe your site and investigate the most common misspellings.

Once you have these common misspellings, add them to your meta tags so that visitors who misspell the meta tags still get a lock to your site.

Adding Meta Tags to Your Web Site

This is the only time that you will ever have to get into the HTML code of your web site because meta tags are written and added to the web site in HTML code.

The fastest easiest and cheapest way to convert the meta tags to an HTML string is to go to www.promotionworld.com. They have a free HTML meta tag string writer that allows you to put in your site description and the meta tags. By simply clicking on a tab, the software will write the HTML string for you.

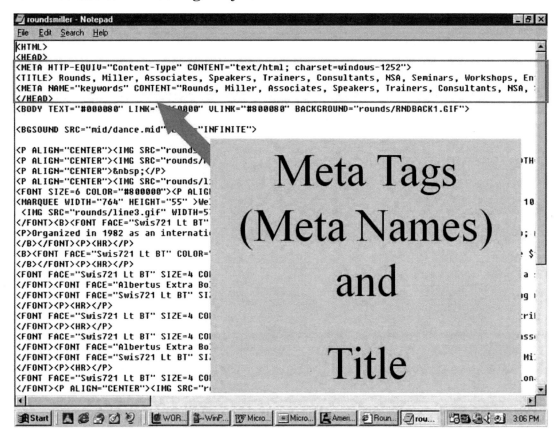

Important note: once you have the meta tag string written by the software, you need to remove any superfluous commands. If you don't remove these commands, the meta tag string will not remain invisible.

To remove the superfluous commands, simply cut and paste the string into the Windows Notepad software. This software will remove the superfluous commands automatically and present you with a hypertext string that you can now cut and paste into your web site.

To add the meta tags to your web site go to the home page of your web site development software and click on the tab that says either code or HTML.

Once you do this, the graphics will disappear and the text-based code will take its place. Notice that at the top of the home page you will find a command called <head>. Simply paste the refined meta tag string onto the home page after the word head. If there is no head command, simply add one before and after the meta tag string.

Now save the page and go back to whatever design or refinement you want to do to your web site.

When you publish your web site to your server, the meta tags will have been inserted and published along with the content and the search engines will index the site as a part of their normal routine.

A quick tip for better meta tag listing. There is a way to get started with meta tag listing that will get you higher on the search engines retrieval list than trying to pick them yourself.

This is accomplished by simply copying the meta tags from the top listed page or pages that you find in the search.

Please note that this is not illegal, immoral, or unethical. But simply a quick and easy method of getting an initial meta tag string for your web site so that you end up in the same proportional location as the sites that you just found.

The process is shown in the diagram:

Step 1. Perform a search for your web page using the words that you think somebody would type in to find your site.

| Step 1 | Step 2 | Step 3 |

Step 2. Using your browser, click on the view command and then select source. Once you have done this, the graphics will disappear and the HTML source code will take its place.

Step 3. Locate the meta tags that are on the top one or two sites that you have found and simply cut and paste the meta tags from these sites into your meta tag string to give you the same series of words and phrases that got this particular site to the top of the search.

There are two serious considerations before you suddenly decide that this is the easiest way to get listed:

1. The person looking for you must still type in the same search words as you typed it and

2. They must be competent in using a search engine.

The bottom line to this entire meta tag selection process is that even though you are conscientious in selecting and installing the meta tags on your web site, there is still no guarantee that the searcher will find you and not somebody else.

Marketing and advertising professionals in today's world will tell you that there is simply no substitute for using conventional advertising and getting your URL into the hands of the searcher so that they type your URL directly and don't spend an inordinate amount of time hunting for you and then find somebody else.

Chapter 4 – How to be an Internet Search Expert

Why is finding something on the net so complicated? You'd think that with everything being completely computerized that it would be easy.

That could be true except for three prime reasons:

1. There is no limit to the amount of information or material that can be stored on the Internet. There are currently estimated to be over 50 billion pages of information on the Internet and millions more are being added each day.

    A physical library has limitations on the amount of material that can be housed within its walls. An electronic library, which is nothing more than a computer with a hard drive, can always add another hard drive or two and triple its capacity for storage in an hour or so.

2. Unlike the libraries that are governed by regulations and how to all use the Dewey Decimal System, the Internet has no formal method of indexing and relies on:

    *   The ingenuity of the people who are writing and shelving their electronic books to index them in a manner that makes sense to us and,

    *   On us, as users, to be clever enough to figure out how the authors of these electronic books think and index their work.

3. There is a reason for the complexity of the Internet's indexing, advertising and commerce.

Conventional paper and ink authors receive their revenues and royalties when a library purchases their book. After that, the number of times their book is checked out and read is of no financial consequence to them.

Web sites are a different story. Since they are used for advertising, promotion, sales, and revenue generation, it's in the best interest to these enterprises to be viewed as often and by as many people as possible.

If they've expended their best efforts to be found on top of the search lists, it'll be their site that is the first one we find when we look for a particular item or topic. Since we find them first, it's more likely that we'll do business with them than with those that are further down the list.

Although this may not seem significant, it's resulted in a listing and ranking battle that confuses everyone and makes it more difficult to find what we're looking for.

The summary of this discussion has been stated simply:

"Imagine that you have one page in one book at the New York Central Library. Somebody tears all the pages from all the books, throws them in a pile on the floor and says—go ahead, find your page, I dare you!" Nancy Miller

In other words, the web has literally become the proverbial needle in the haystack. As a result, the Internet and more specifically the web needs a tool to help us find what we're looking for and to help others to find us.

These tools are called search engines. There are over 100 general-purpose search engines in widespread use and thousands of topic specific engines. These engines search the entire Internet looking for web sites, FTP sites, gopher sites, and USENET newsgroups.

Each engine searches in a slightly different fashion, so the search results will be different with each search engine.

No engine is better than another—just different. As you begin to use them, you'll probably decide on a favorite or two. Later on we'll introduce slave drivers that will allow you to command multiple engines to search simultaneously.

All current Internet packages allow access to many different search engines that look for a variety of variables, but the primary search criteria is for a series of profile or key words that are posted in a hidden file when the web page or pages are posted in cyberspace.

HOW TO USE SEARCH ENGINES

All search engines appear to have some proprietary gimmick that's supposed to make them easier to use than the others.

Here are some other operating guidelines for obtaining maximum efficiency from search engines.

Search engines understand plain English and are programmed with novice users in mind so you don't need to be a master of Boolean search syntax to unleash their power.

To use the engines search feature, you need to be able to describe what you're looking for with a series of words or a phrase. Type those words into the search box, click on the search button, and the search engine will find resources on the web that match your search.

First, there are several different types of search engines:

1. Site engine—It's like an electronic table of contents for a specific net publication because it only searches within its boundaries.

2. Directory engine—These are topic specific engines that are focused on subjects like magazines, bicycles, clip art, or criminal law.

3. Shopping engines—These are designed to help us locate and purchase specific goods and services.

4. General-Purpose Search Engines—These are the most widely known and although they are popular because of their general characteristics and flexibility, aren't necessarily the most efficient way to locate something.

5. Meta Search or Slave Driver Engine—These are devices that actually become masters to a multitude of general-purpose slave engines and command several of them to search for the same thing simultaneously.

Logically, the easiest and most comprehensive search engines are the ones near the top that are already predisposed to finding what we're looking for and the least user-friendly are the general-purpose engines on the bottom.

We'll be showing you how to use all of these tools and we'll even make the general-purpose engines easy to use and very efficient.

Site Engines

The first real search engine is the site engine.

If you already know the URL of a site, or after you locate and are about to enter a specific site, this engine will act as an electronic table of contents that'll jump you to exactly what you're looking for within the site.

A good example of a site engine is on the site for one of the world's largest home supply firms, Home Depot(www.homedepot.com). Notice that they have a search engine that searches for items ONLY within the confines of their site.

Topic Specific Engines

If you know the general topic you want to locate, a topic specific engine is the best way to find what you're looking for.

The topic specific search engines have their own electronic index and the best master index we've found for topic specific search engines is at www.refdesk.com.

At RefDesk, you'll find thousands of linked topic specific search tools that will take you directly to the sites that contain the information you're looking for.

For example, the web is loaded with pictures and other graphics. Ditto (www.ditto.com) is a topic specific search engine that is specifically designed to assist you in locating sources of graphic arts, cartoons, and clip art.

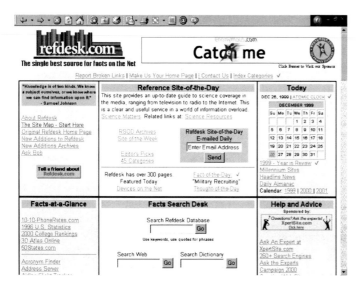

One of the best features of Ditto is that it's been configured for general-purpose usage and automatically filters out material that might be considered objectionable to children.

In our example, we've typed in the word bicycles and asked it to locate pictures and drawings of bicycles for us.

I spend a lot of time on the road so here's one of my favorites (and if you do much traveling at all, I'll bet it'll be one of yours too!) www.mapquest.com.

Rather than to head down to the auto club, you can enter the addresses of the start and finish of your trip. Then, it'll automatically create a turn-by-turn driving map from start to finish complete with all of the mileages between the reference points.

You can print out the driving directions to take along and for those who are using the Palm type computers, this site also downloads driving instructions into your hand-held computer so you read it from the display.

People in my seminars want to locate someone on the Internet—a friend, relation, school chum, or military buddy. www.WhoWhere.com is a search engine that will assist you in finding people.

General-Purpose Search Engines

Since most of us are going to use general-purpose search engines, we need to spend some additional time explaining how they work. There are roughly 150 general-purpose search engines available to us on the Internet.

Since technology keeps changing and evolving, there is never a permanent best search engine since the major ones keep improving and leapfrogging over the competition.

The international directory of the current search engines is located at www.searchenginecolossus.com. From this site you can select the engine that appeals to your search style or your specific needs.

Importance of Key Words

Before we go any further, we need to have a discussion about the words that you'll be typing in the search windows. It was important in the topic specific and protocol engines, but it's critical in the general-purpose engines.

Why? Because they're general-purpose and the words used to define what we're looking for will determine the accuracy of the search.

In the engines we described previously, the categories and some of the topics were already pre-defined and specified. This left us with a limited number of choices and made the search easier.

Now we're dealing with a wide-open search engine that will literally look for anything, anywhere on the Internet without any pre-disposition or categories.

This means that it's up to you to put definition and direction in your search terms or the results will be disastrous. It also means that you're going to have to think like the person who created and stored the information because they're the one's who indexed it.

First, let's look at how search engines actually search for something.

If the site's author has properly indexed a site, especially a web site, it will have three different things that the search engine can key into:

1. The key words. They're also known as meta tags and index words. These are the words that the site's author figured you or I would type in to find the site. They are stored in a hidden file on the home page and only the search engine sees them.

2. Titles and descriptions. This is the headline on the home page or it can also be a hidden file that only the search engine can see.

3. All the words in a site. This is just what it means. Engines that search every word or phrase in a site are known as meta search engines although more and more of the engines are looking at the words in the home page as a standard practice.

Now let's look at how search engines index the Internet.

First of all, there are currently estimated to be in excess of 50 billion pages of information available to us on the Internet.

It would be virtually impossible for a search engine to search all of the computers and all of the pages each time someone asks for a search to be performed. Instead, each search engine maintains its own database of information about the sites on the Internet—sort of like its own card catalog.

When you and your computer ask for a search, the engine checks through its own database and comes up with the sites that match the specified search criteria.

The index information is loaded into the database in two ways:

1. Each search engine has a gadget called a spider robot that spends its entire existence indexing or spidering web sites. Since each engine operates a little differently from the others, the indexing information varies from one engine to another.

    Sites that have only been spidered suffer from two problems:

    a) The indexing information is based on the spider robot's programmed instructions for gathering and indexing site information and

   b) The spiders have a tough time getting around to all the sites especially when you consider that over 50 percent of them get changed annually.

2. The second way a site gets indexed is when the author of the site takes the time and trouble to create a set of meta tags and description and submits it to each of the search engines independently. In other words, the author tells the engine how the site is to be listed (for a fee, of course!).

Although this sounds great, many site authors are either ignorant of what needs to be done to properly index their site with the engines or they are simply not motivated to do it properly or sometimes at all. Regardless of the reason, the results for a searcher can be disastrous. When the site isn't indexed properly, the person searching for it can't find it.

Let's look at a specific example and what we, as search experts, can do about it. Let's suppose that a company specializes in toilet repair.

Most site authors use the Yellow Pages mentality, which is the only experience that most of the world has ever had in picking a classification, heading, or topic under which they would be found.

The logical terms that most of us list ourselves under are: toilet, repair and perhaps even toilet and repair. This sounds OK but most people would look under plumbing.

In fact, here are several popular terms that we use to describe a toilet and these are not all encompassing: toilet, head, restroom, washroom, lounge, men's room, ladies room, crapper, john, sandbox, little girls room, lavatory, potty, and little boys room.

Although toilet repair may seem a little crude as an example, I chose it because we all know what a toilet is and so far, I've located over 100 different words that we use to describe one. If anyone searching for the toilet repair site uses a word that isn't indexed, they won't find the site.

Most of the site authors do NOT bother to come up with all the possible variations for their indexing. The problem lies in the excessive number of possibilities for indexing and the lack of conscientious effort on the part of the site authors to be comprehensive in their indexing.

What this boils down to is if you can't find what you're looking for, use a thesaurus and try variations on the topic, theme or descriptive words. You'll be surprised at how well it works.

Merriam-Webster's electronic thesaurus site, www.M-W.com will help you locate a variety of words to use in your searches.

BOOLEAN SEARCH PROCESS

Before you use any search engine, print out the advanced search instructions.

Although most of the engines all do the same things, the commands for doing them vary from engine to engine. To make sure you're telling the engine the right thing to do, you need these instructions. They're usually listed under help and Advanced Search Instructions.

Experience has shown that the BEST way to use a search engine is to properly use the Boolean search functions that are programmed into it. Here's how the Boolean search concept works:

1. Decide on the key words that you want to look for. These are usually the most common way a product, service, company, or topic would be listed or asked for.

2. Go to a search engine and enter the key words that you are looking for.

3. Review the Boolean search instructions and configure the search accordingly.

4. Perform the search.

The Boolean search criteria that the engines use are the basic language of computers. It allows a specified string of words, like girls tandem bicycles and can ask the engine to search for sites or pages that contain one or all of the specified words.

For example, if you specify OR then you'll get any page that contains girls, or tandem, or bicycle.

If you specify AND then you'll only get the pages that contain girls and tandem and bicycle and the list will be smaller and tighter.

The Boolean Commands

AND: tandem AND bicycle—Locates pages that include both of the words. For example pages containing both tandem and bicycle.

OR: tandem OR bicycle—Locates pages that include either of the words or both. For example pages containing tandem or those containing bicycle or those containing both tandem and bicycle. Most search engines perform "or" searching by default so it is not necessary to explicitly specify an "or" search.

NOT: tandem NOT bicycle—Pages that include the first word but not the second. For example pages containing tandem but not bicycle.

NEAR: tandem NEAR/25 bicycle—Locates pages in which both words appear within 25 words of each other in either direction. If you do not specify a range, as in the example, tandem near bicycle, the search will return pages in which the two words are next to each other (in either order).

ADJ (adjacent): tandem ADJ bicycle—Locates pages in which the two words appear next to each other in that order. For example pages containing tandem bicycle.

"..." "tandem bicycle"—Locates pages containing the phrase. For example only those documents containing the phrase "tandem bicycle." For two word phrases such as tandem bicycle, tandem ADJ bicycle has the same effect.

(...) tandem NOT/ (bicycle or bus)—Pages containing the first word NOT either of the other two. For example pages containing tandem but NOT tandem bicycle or tandem bus. Parentheses simplify the creation of complex queries and can be used in combination with any of the search operators on this list.

Slave Driver Engines

For as good as search engines are and what they will become, they cannot search and find something that is not listed in their indices.

> Slave Driver Engines
> www.google.com
> www.mamma.com
> www.ask.com
> www.Go.com

Because of the growing number of search engines, the time and complexity involved with listing sites with the different engines, and the lack of a central organization system like the Dewey Decimal System, most sites are only listed with a select number of engines and these are usually the personal preference of the owner of the site.

Because of this, according to the Wall Street Journal, "No search engine currently available searches more than 20 percent of the net and most only search 5-to 8 percent."

The answer to performing a comprehensive search lies is the use of a device called a meta search engine. These are often refereed to as slave driver engines because they become the master and other engines are slaved to their commands.

Simplistically, they take the search criteria specified and make multiple requests of several search engines and then compile and refine the results for the searcher.

The results are a dramatic improvement over the use of single engines because each engine's index is different. Some of the meta search engines search the indices of over 100 search engines simultaneously.

As with just about everything on the Internet, meta search engines have their own index site where you can pick, choose, and hot link yourself to the engine of your choice.

In this case, the URL is www.reverse-lookup.com. You'll find yourself right in the middle of a hot linked list of the most powerful search tools on the Internet—slave driver engines.

Time Saving Techniques

Unless your occupation is Internet searching, you're probably not real interested in spending any more time than you have to in the actual searching itself. What you're interested in are the results.

For as great as these techniques are for finding the sites, there's still the matter of the time required to review the sites to see which ones have relevant information and which is of little or no value to us especially if you're using a modem.

In this section, we'll review five super techniques for cutting your search and download time by up to 80 percent of what you've currently been expending.

1. The first time saver is to always bring back the summaries on your searches. Every one of the engines will give you the choice of listing the title of the site or a short summary—always choose the summaries—here's why.

   Think about going to a video store. You spot a flashy cover with an intriguing title and say to yourself: "This looks like the one I want." Then, you turn over the video and read the description and discover that it's really not what you were looking for.

   You just saved yourself the cost of rental along with a waste of time.

   Summaries from searches do the same thing—they allow us to review the primary contents of a site and make a decision as to whether or not we want to invest our time in a thorough review of the site.

   Obviously, if the summary shows nothing relevant, we probably won't waste our time reviewing the site.

   There's another reason that's becoming prevalent—language differences. Over 40 percent of the web is posted in a language other than English. The title may not be indicative of this but the summary will be.

   Once again, we've used the summary to prevent us from a time wasting effort.

2. Here's a neat trick that we can all do, but usually don't—turn off the graphics on the first search.

   Why? Because graphics take from 2 to 800 time longer to download than text due to compression, conversion, translation, and display.

   The secret is to do your first search with the graphics turned off so you won't have to wait forever for graphics to download and display.

   When you do this, you'll see a little box that indicates where the graphic belongs.

   Review the site and see if there's anything of interest. If there is, and you don't need the graphics, or if their isn't, you've saved yourself a lot of time by not having to wait for them.

   To turn off the graphics on your browser, click on the help screen and type in graphics. One of the notes will tell you, step-by-step, how to turn them off and on.

3. You're probably asking yourself: "How do I jump between graphics on and graphics off?" This is our third tip—set a bookmark.

   As you review sites with the graphics turned off, bookmark the sites that you believe have useful information or interesting graphics.

   After you've marked the sites you want, turn the graphics back on, click the refresh button, and ONLY revisit the sites you've marked.

   In Internet Explorer, look for the command *Favorites* on the top toolbar. Then, click *Add to Favorites*. In Netscape Navigator, use the command *Bookmarks*, and in AOL, use the command for *Favorite Places*.

4. No matter what operating system you're using today, it has the inherent capability to multitask. That means that it can do two or more things at the same time and that includes operate a search engine.

   Here's an example of how it's done and what it'll do for you. First activate the browser by clicking on its icon. When the screen fills with the image of the browser, use your mouse and pull the screen back from right to left so that it only utilizes 50 percent of the entire viewing area.

   Then activate the browser a second time. This time, when the image fills the screen, use your mouse and pull the screen from left to right and let it fill the right 50 percent of the screen.

   You now have your browser activated twice and it can be set to address the same site or two different sites at the same time.

In this example, I'm looking at www.Ditto.com, the search engine site that locates graphics. While I'm searching for graphics that I want to download on one of the browser screens, I'm actually downloading on the other. When the download process is complete, I simply reverse the roles of the browsers and download from one while searching the other.

This simple technique will guarantee you a 50 percent reduction in waiting and downloading time for any site or information you require.

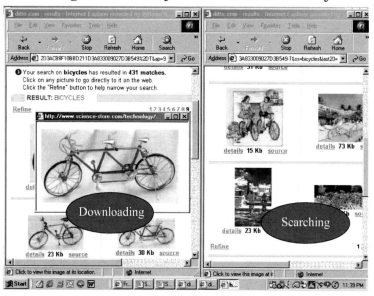

5. Save the site for later review. Some web sites are huge and take a long time to download. Rather than wait for the process to be completed, you can program your browser to download and save a site's information while you're doing something else that's useful and productive, like sleeping.

Think of this as something like TIVO for your computer—a system that let's you record sites and view them at a later time.

There are several programs, FREE and fee that perform this function including SurfSaver (www.surfsaver.com). The fastest way, however, is to use the built in features of your browser. Both Internet Explorer and Netscape Navigator have the ability.

Learn the process of programming your browser to save sites for you to review later from your hard drive, click on help and look under Saving Pages For Off-line Viewing. You'll find step-by-step instructions for setting them up to save sites for you at whatever time you specify, even while you're sleeping.

Recommended Reference and Update Material

Nothing in this high-speed access world of the Internet stays the same for very long. If you expect to maintain your proficiency as a search expert, you'll have to visit some reference sites on a regular basis to see what's new and what's changed.

Here are two of the BEST reference sites we've found for staying current in the world of efficient searches.

Search Engine Watch (www.Searchenginewatch.com) keeps track of what's current in search technology and usually publishes the latest and greatest techniques as they are released.

They have a tutorial on understanding search engines, a search primer on the Boolean functions, an index of search engines, and a set of conclusions based on their research and findings.

Although many things we've shown you so far was FREE, it was, for the most part, located somewhere on the net.

In other words, you are actually time sharing software with the world. If you are interested in FREE, proprietary software programs to install on your computer that will aid you with your searches, this is the place to go.

Ziff Davis, the publishing firm, has located and compiled a great list of software that's FREE and easy to use (http://Downloads.zdnet.com).

Hooked on Google?

If you're like most people these days, you probably log on to www.google.com or www.yahoo.com and rely on these search tools to do the work for you.

Depending on whom you ask, Google accounts for between 40 and 60 percent of the search engine market. And rightly so—the service gives speedy results and has a very good user interface. If you add in Yahoo! and MSN, the top three search engines have around 90 percent of the market.

But don't you ever want to try a different search engine, just to see where it takes you? After all, Google's search results are based on relevance and popularity, so scrolling through Google results isn't the best way to get off the beaten path and discover new web territory.

Here are a few ways to break your addiction and still find exactly what you need.

1. Technorati (www.technorati.com) If you're not including BLOGs in your web searches, you're missing out on a ton of great content that is often too

recent to be near the top of typical search results, which skew toward popularity instead of timeliness. Among Google alternatives here, the best one we've seen is Technorati. The BLOG—search service includes plenty of ways to search for the hottest BLOG content, including a Top Searches list, a list of the most-linked-to BLOGs, and the music, movies, videos, and games that most BLOGgers are linking to. Searching is easy, and you can sort results by timeliness (for the newest content) or authority (BLOGs with more inbound links have more authority).

2. ChaCha (www.chacha.com) Can't find what you're looking for? ChaCha search lets you chat with a real live professional guide who takes your query and returns related results tailor made to your specifications. The service is quirky enough to be a lot of fun, and it's completely free.

3. Rollyo (www.rollyo.com) Short for Roll Your Own Search Engine, Rollyo lets you do just that. You can do general searches or category searches to get results from BLOGs and the web at large, or create your own search engine (or Searchroll) to search only specific sites. For instance, I created a Searchroll that searches only my favorite music BLOGs. You can view other users Searchrolls including celebrity search rolls. There aren't many instances in which I'd want to limit the number of sites I'm searching, but if that's your thing, Rollyo definitely makes it easy.

4. Kosmix (www.kosmix.com) This topical search engine conducts searches by category: health, autos, travel, finance, politics, and video games. On timely issues, its results are pretty terrible and often outdated, so it was tricky to test its effectiveness on search terms other than broad issues such as *campaign financing* or *global warming*. The paid search results on it are much more timely and relevant. Kosmix results fared much better with less time-sensitive issues and search terms. On health topics it delivered lots of information on prevention.

5. Clusty (www.clusty.com) The unfortunately named Clusty takes a different approach to search results. Whereas Google arranges your results in a simple list, Clusty first aggregates the results from several search engines (Google not included), then arranges them in clusters to help you further refine your search. For instance, a search for *Dell XPS* returns clusters such as various XPS model numbers, reviews, and shopping links with prices.

6. Ask.com (www.Ask.com) This incredibly feature-rich site uses a process called subject specific popularity, which means that instead of ordering results simply by popularity, it orders them by "popularity among pages considered to be experts pick of your search."

7. StumbleUpon (www.stumbleupon.com) StumbleUpon gives you thumbs-up/thumbs-down icons in your toolbar and lets you rate pages and sites you come across. As it learns your preferences, it gets better at directing you to stuff you'll like. You can add other people with similar interests. It

will further refine your search results. The site can be slow at times, but it's a great way to find web content you wouldn't be exposed to otherwise.

8. Draze Meta Search (www.draze.com) This site lets you collects search results quickly from Google, MSN and Yahoo!. The home page looks like a typical Google page, with a search bar. You can also choose to view the results.

   The results page includes a Peek-a-Boo feature that gives you full, scrollable page previews, and you don't have to click through to a page to see that it isn't helpful.

Chapter 5 – The Law and the Internet

This section is NOT intended to be a course in Internet law, but it is included so you'll get a relative idea of how the web is covered by conventional (and sometime unconventional) legal practices.

LIBEL AND SLANDER

The definitions of libel and slander are as follows:

Libel: Any malicious defamation, expressed either in printing, writing, pictures, or effigies, which sets a person in an odious or ridiculous light and thereby diminishes his/her reputation.

Slander: The utterance of false, malicious, and defamatory words to the damage of another.

Although we are primarily only dealing with the libel laws on the Internet because virtually everything TODAY is expressed in writing or graphics, we are entering the era of sending voice mail messages and the slander laws now take effect with equal meaning and content.

INTERNET LEGAL TIPS

Despite the legal risks involved, we believe that businesses can steer clear of trouble if they take proper precautions. If you're planning on doing any business on the Internet, here are some legal tips offered by intellectual property lawyers.

Get it in writing. Unless you're using a digital signature system, ask the customer or contractor to send you a signed paper original or a fax. Because of security and authentication problems, e-mail should not be used to create a contract.

Watch what you say (type, that is). As matter of law, it usually doesn't matter which medium was used to transmit allegedly defamatory material. Even letters and telegrams have been considered sufficient, says Hillary Miller, an attorney who participates in CompuServe's Legal Forum. "There is every reason to include electronic media within the scope of those media capable of use for the commission of a tort of defamation, particularly given the potential for immediate and widespread dissemination of information to a targeted audience where substantial harm can be inflicted," Miller says.

Translation: Post something really nasty online and prepare to be sued.

Recognize that the laws that apply in the real world will probably be applied to cyberspace as well. This is particularly true of laws involving trademark and copyright infringement.

TRADEMARK AND COPYRIGHT LAW

With the widespread proliferation of computers, scanners, optical character readers (OCR), videotape interface, and other emerging technology, it has become quite easy to rip off another person or firm's legally protected material.

Both trademark and copyright are covered under the Federal forgery and counterfeiting laws, so it's not an insignificant matter if you are charged with violations of these laws.

Trademark law covers the recognizable elements of a company's goods or services. These include the look, logo, package design, or trade name. Trademarks are valuable because we don't buy things these days based on the product or service itself as much as we do on their recognizable packaging or advertising characteristics.

When you copy or deceptively imitate the trademark of another firm, you're practicing a form of fraud because you are, in effect, telling the potential customer that you are someone that you are not.

Copyright covers the actual embodied work of a creative individual or group. Covered are written work, music, art, software, graphics, clip art, pantomime, choreographic routines, dance steps, sports play books, audio and video recordings and more.

Like trademarks, copyrights are Federally protected and great care should be taken to ensure that the work you copy and use is not the property of another.

The Patent and Trademark Office in Washington, DC will send you a copy of the trademark application forms for FREE. In this packet of information are all of the basic rules and regulations governing trademark law. The Copyright Office in Washington, DC will send you the materials for FREE if you ask them.

Reproducible Isn't Necessarily Reproducible!

Just because you have the ability through copy machines, scanners, computers and other pieces of technology to copy something that somebody else has created does not mean you have the right to make copies. The rules, regulations and laws governing trademarks and copyrights have been developed and are enforced to protect both those who create the work and those who are at effect of the work.

WARRANTIES

Warranties and exchanges are a matter of policy rather than matter of the law. However, the law states that you must live up to the representation that is made. They come under the truth in advertising laws and basically states that what you represent in your advertising becomes the contractual guidelines that both you and the customer must abide by.

It's subjective in nature but common sense and ethics regarding doing the best you can for the customer appears to be the ground rule for success in the foreseeable future.

CONTRACT LAW

Advertising is the representation that you make. If you do not live up to that representation, you are in breach of contract. Advertising is a form of contractual law. It is a contract between you, the seller of goods and the recipient of goods.

If you advertise a recipe booklet on the Internet that has 50 recipes for $20, you have established the ground rules for the transaction.

If a customer sends you $20 and you send the 50 recipes, you're completed the order. However, if you only sent 49 recipes, you would be in breach. The customer has three choices:

1. Demand their money back, with no penalty to them.

2. Demand that you complete the order at no cost to them.

3. Allow a substitution of equal or comparable value.

DELIVERY

Rules of the Federal Trade Commission (FTC) and various state laws govern Internet sales. In general, these guidelines are:

The seller must ship the customer's order within 30 days or one calendar month (whichever is greater) of receiving the order, unless the advertisement clearly states something different [for example 4-6 weeks].

If it appears that the customer's order will not be shipped when promised, the seller must notify the customer in writing in advance of the promised date, giving a definite new date, if known and offering the customer the opportunity to cancel the order with a refund or consent to a definite delayed shipping date or an indefinite delay.

The seller's notice must contain a stamped self-addressed card or envelope [even a toll FREE number] with which to indicate the customer's preference. If the customer does not respond to this notice, the seller may assume the customer agrees to the delay, but must either ship or cancel the customer's order within 30 days after the original shipping date promised or required. A prompt refund must be made when an order is canceled.

Even if the customer has consented to an indefinite delay, the customer retains the right to cancel the order at any time before the item has been shipped.

If the customer chooses to cancel an order that has been paid for by check or money order, the seller must mail the customer a refund within seven business days. If the customer cancels an order for which the customer paid by credit card, the seller must credit the customer's account within one billing cycle following receipt of the customer's request.

In the event that the item the customer ordered is unavailable, the seller may not send the customer substitute merchandise without the customer's express consent.

One of the problems in doing this is that a great deal of direct response purchasing on the Internet is done on impulse. People who order now— want it now!

Chapter 6 – Tips and Resources

To support your continued learning, we've researched some of the most useful reference sites and material about the Internet and its associated topics.

We've divided it into categories to make it easy to find and use the most valuable reference points. Most of the software is FREE but some of the utilities cost a few dollars.

First, here are some keyboard tips to help you surf the net easier. While you're online, use these keyboard combinations to streamline your efforts:

Keyboard tips and tricks to make your Internet Surfin' experience more enjoyable.

CTRL A—Blocks all the information on a web page for copying.

CTRL B—Brings up your bookmarks for maintenance and additions (Explorer and Navigator).

CTRL C—Copies the blocked content to the clipboard.

CTRL F—Brings up a search engine to search the content of ANY web page (Explorer, Navigator and AOL).

CTRL H—Brings up the history of where you've been for past several weeks (Explorer and Navigator).

CTRL I—Brings up the Favorites list (Bookmarks) (Explorer and Navigator).

CTRL L—Opens a web folder or URL.

CTRL O—Opens a web folder or URL.

CTRL P—Prints the content of the current web page.

CTRL V—Pastes the copy stored on the clipboard.

F11—Expands the view of your browser to full screen and back again (Explorer and Navigator).

ALT + TAB—Brings up a panel of active programs so you can switch from one to another.

WINDOWS HELP KEYS

Most of the recent keyboards come with a Windows key. Here are the special commands that this magic key invokes:

Feature	Keystrokes
display the start menu	⊞
open the run dialog box	⊞ R
minimize all	⊞ M
undo minimize all, tile horizontally, tile vertically, or cascade	⊞ <Shift> M
open help	⊞ F1
open windows explorer	⊞ E
open find/search files or folders	⊞ F
minimize all and undo minimize all	⊞ D
cycle through the taskbar buttons	<Alt> <Tab>
open system properties sheet	⊞ <Break>
display the shortcut menu for the selected item	<Application>

ERROR CODES EXPLAINED

If you've ever wondered what those error codes mean, here's what they're all about and what YOU SHOULD do. If your screen says:

"401 Unauthorized" IT MEANS you need a password to get into the site. YOU SHOULD try retyping your password if you are supposed to have access to the site. If you don't, stop trying and go somewhere else.

"404 Error: Page is no longer available" IT MEANS the part of the page you're looking for is no longer there or that part of the URL is wrong. YOU SHOULD not give up. First check the URL. If it's right, it's possible that the content moved to another part of the site and the site managers didn't define a redirect. Try deleting the end part of the URL to see if that gets you to a workable page. Or see if the site has an internal search engine you can use to find the content.

"503: Service unavailable" IT MEANS you have a temporary problem on your hands, like the server of the site you're trying to access is down. YOU SHOULD cheer up. Try again in a few minutes.

WHO WORKS WITH WHOM IN THE US SEARCH ENGINE MARKET?

(Courtesy of Attach USA www.attachusa.com)

Search engines and directories interrelate with other search engines; for instance, they share their database contents to cover more web pages. In addition, the search engines partner with pay per click search engines to supplement their revenue.

It's essential to know which search engines and directories work together. If you want to plan an effective search engine optimization strategy, you must know which search engines cooperate and who gets results from whom.

- AllTheweb—Gets search results from FAST Search and paid results from Overture.

- AltaVista—Has its own database but gets directory results from the Open Directory Project and paid results from Overture.

- AOL Search—Gets normal search results and paid results from Google, as well as directory results from the Open Directory Project.

- Ask—Has its own database but gets additional results from Teoma and paid results from Google.

- Google—Has its own database but gets directory results from the Open Directory Project.

- HotBot—Gets search results from Inktomi, directory results from the Open Directory Project and paid results from Google. HotBot can also display unfiltered search results from Ask, Google and Lycos.

- Inktomi—Has its own database.

- iWon—Gets search results Google, directory results from the Open Directory Project and paid results from Google.

- LookSmart—Has its own database but gets additional results from Inktomi.

- Lycos—Gets search results from FAST Search, directory results from the Open Directory Project and paid results from Google.

- MSN Search—Gets search results from Inktomi and LookSmart. MSN Search is currently working on its own database.

- Netscape Search—Gets search results from Google, directory results from the Open Directory project and paid results from Google.

- Overture—Has its own database but gets additional results from Inktomi.

- Teoma—Has its own database but gets directory results from the Open Directory Project.

- Yahoo!—Has its own human-compiled database but gets addition results from Google and paid results from Overture. Yahoo! owns AllTheweb, AltaVista and Inktomi so it will probably switch in the near future from Google to the results of its own companies.

Statistics:

www.clickin.com   www.jup.com
www.cyberatlas.com   www.nua.ie/surveys
www.find.com   www.pcmeter.com
www.forrester.com   www.survey.net
www.idc.com   www.thestandard.com

General Reference Sites

Acronym Finder www.acronymfinder.com
Webster's Hypertext Dictionary/thesaurus http://m-w.com/netdict.htm
Bartlett's familiar quotations www.columbia.edu/acis/bartleby/bartlett/
Roget's online Thesaurus www.thesaurus.com
Onelook—79 dictionaries, etc www.onelook.com
Electric Library www.elibrary.com
Internet Public Library www.ipl.com
Master Library Index at http://sunsite.berkeley.edu/Libweb
The quotations page www.starlingtech.com/quotes.index.html
Toll Free Directory www.tollfree.att.net
ZIP code lookup and address information www.usps.gov/ncsc
Area Codes http://www.555-1212.com/ACLOOKUP.htmlwww.555-1212.com/geo.jsp
Who's Who—15,000 people worth knowing www.biography.com
Learn how to www.refdesk.com
Finding Articles www.findarticles.com/cf_0/PI/subject.jhtml
Fact Checker www.bartleby.com/reference
Almanac Information www.infoplease.com/almanacs.html
Accurate time www.timeticker.com
Colleges and Universities www.google.com/options/universities.html

E-MAIL SUPPORT SITES

FREE web based e-mail:

www.altavista.com   www.hotmail.com

www.amexmail.com   www.juni.com

www.briefcase.com   www.lycos.com

www.crosswinds.net   www.netaddress.net

www.deskmail.com   www.whalemail.com

www.excite.com   www.yahoo.com

FREE e-mail and text translation software:

http://babelfish.altavista.com   www.freetranslation.com

www.altavista.com   www.google.com

FREE e-mail phonebooks and lookup directories:

http://people.yahoo.com   www.phonenumbers.net

www.411locate.com   www.refdesk.com/instant.html

www.bigfoot.com   www.startingpage.com/html/looku

www.bigyellow.com   p.html

www.freeality.com/finde.htm   www.switchboard.com

www.iaf.net   www.theultimates.com

www.inter800.com   www.whowhere.com

www.nedsite.nl/search/people.htm   www.worldpages.com/global

E-mail graphic and speech enhancement tools:

www.4developers.com/talkmail   www.talkingcallerid.com/default.ht

www.bonzi.com   m

www.sonicmail.com   www.togglethis.com

Anti-spam and junk mail:

http://www.e-mailanywhere.com

http://www.mail2web.com

www.bomis.com/rings/spam

www.computerlinkmag.com/articles/mar2000/spam.htm

www.exit109.com/~jeremy/news/antispam.html

www.spamkiller.com

www.webmasterfree.com/eater.html

Stop "Pop up" www.Panicware.com

Outlook/Outlook Express *I Hate Spam* $20 www.sunbeltsoftware.com

Objectionable site blocking software:

www.browsesafe.com

www.cyberpatrol.com

www.netnanny.com

www.owt.com/software/blockers.html

Free auto responders:
www.thebusinessguide.org
www.ismy.net/autoresponders.html
www.sendfree.com/tips.htm
www.onlinesuccesstips.com/articles/autoresponders

Security for your system:
Free anti-virus program http://antivirus.cai.com
Security testing software www.pcflank.com

SEARCH TOOLS AND DIRECTORIES

Slave Driver (multi-engine) engines (Note: single search engines only search their own internal card catalogs. Meta search engines search the catalogs of dozens, even hundreds of the major search engine catalogs simultaneously and compile a comprehensive list for you):

http://www.gocee.com/eureka	www.cyber411.com
http://www.onekey.com	www.dogpile.com
www.allnetresearch.com	www.go.com
www.ask.com	www.google.com
www.askme.com	www.mamma.com
www.copernic.com	www.search.com
www.cs.colostate.edu	www.vivisimo.com

The best and most comprehensive directories for finding people and businesses:
http://www.yellownet.com
www.bigbook.com
www.bizstats.com

Special interest search tools and directories business:
www.corporateinformation.com
City Guides/Shopping www.smartpages.com
General www.searchability.com
General www.addsheet.com/search/ospecial.html
http://www.lairgauche.com/engines.htm
General www.virtualfreesites.com/search.html
General www.cyward.com/speciali.htm
Business and Corporate Information www.ecompany.com

Topic specific search engine indices:

http://www.searchtopics.com	www.search.com
www.askme.com	www.searchbug.com
www.ehow.com	www.searchit.net
www.howstuffworks.com	www.weeno.com
www.learn2.com	www.leidenuniv.nl/ub/biv/specials.
www.Refdesk.com	htm

Chapter 7 – Glossary

ARPANET: Advanced Research Projects Agency where the theories and software on which the Internet is based were tested.

ASCII American Standard Code for Information Interchange: An ASCII file contains only alphanumeric characters and is universally accepted by every software program.

Autoresponder or MailBot: This is a text file that is sent automatically back to someone who sends an e-mail message requesting it.

Baud: A measure of modem speed. The higher the baud speed of the modem, the more information that can be transmitted per unit of time.

Browser: A translation program that converts the information received from the net (and especially the web) into usable images and sounds. Current browsers are complete tools kits with several functions combined into their structure.

Chat: A service that allows two or more people to have an electronic conversation, or a real-time online conference call over the Internet.

Compression: The process of squeezing data to eliminate redundancies and allow files to be stored in less space. Often files are archived and transmitted in a compressed format to save space and transmission time.

Cookie: A method used on web sites to track visitors. Cookies are designed to recognize a user's ID or password when they revisit a site.

Cyberspace: Often used in reference to the nowhere universe of networked computers where things happen online.

Download: To retrieve information from the Internet.

DSL Digital Subscriber Lines: Digital implementation of the POTS lines to provide high speed data access. Current speeds are dependent on distance the subscriber is from the telephone relays station.

E-mail or Electronic mail: One of the most used functions of the Internet—it is essentially a messaging system.

FAQ: A list of Frequently Asked Questions and their answers.

Firewall: A system that sits between a site's internal network and the Internet to restrict certain types of traffic from passing between them.

Flame: An angry response or largely personal attack against someone with opposing views or someone who has violated Netiquette.

Freeware: Software that can be distributed freely and used for FREE, but for which the author often retains the copyright.

FTP File Transfer Protocol: A software application that enables the transfer of files to or from a remote computer onto your computer.

GIF: A method used to compress and transfer graphics images into digital information.

Hit: A way of measuring the number of visitors to a web site or the number of responses received when a search is performed.

Home page: A document that is displayed when first entering a web site. It is a home base to start from.

HTML HyperText Markup Language: The language of web documents.

HTTP HyperText Transfer Protocol: A protocol or language used by www servers and clients to transfer HTML documents.

Hyperlink: An icon, graphic, or word in a file that when clicked with the mouse, automatically jumps to another preprogrammed site and opens that file for viewing.

Hypertext: Refers to the linkage of one document to another through movement instructions attached to selected words and images.

IRC Internet Relay Chat: A worldwide network of people talking to each other in real time over the Internet rather than in person. See chat.

ISDN Integrated Services Digital Network: A four-wire system for providing 128 kbps services to industrial locations.

ISP Internet Service Provider: An organization that provides connections to the Internet, usually based on a monthly and/or hourly fee, for the end user. Commonly referred to as a service provider.

JPEG: A digital method used to compress and transfer graphics images.

LISTSERV: An automated program for managing mailing lists. It is essentially an electronic pen pal club.

Modem: A device that allows your computer to talk to another computer or the Internet via the phone lines.

Net: A short way of referring to the Internet.

Netiquette: Internet etiquette, a set of operating conventions and codes of behavior you are expected to follow while online.

Newsgroup: An automated message area in which subscribers post messages to the entire group on specific topics.

Off-line: The state of not being connected to the Internet.

Online: The state of being connected to the Internet.

Password: The secret string of characters assigned to your individual login name on a particular system. It prevents others from accessing the computer accounts.

Post: To place a message on a bulletin board, in a forum or in a Usenet newsgroup for public reading.

POTS Plain Old Telephone Service: The conventional copper wires that are used for voice communications.

Router: A computer system that makes decisions about which path Internet traffic will take to reach its destination.

Service Provider: A company or other entity that provides Internet or other computer services to a third party. See ISP.

Shareware: Software available on a trial basis at no cost from FTP sites. After the trial period, users are required to register and send in registration fees, which entitle them to documentation, technical support and program upgrades.

Signature file (.sig file): A file, typically between four and eight lines long, that users append to the end of their electronic mail, Usenet newsgroup or mailing list message postings. It's a good way to get a promotional message out about your business or yourself without offending Internet users with blatant advertising. This is sometimes referred to as an electronic business card.

Snail mail: The standard name on the Internet for paper mail, because e-mail can travel across the world in seconds, and paper mail takes days.

Spamming: The act of sending hundreds of inappropriate postings to BLOGS, USENET newsgroups and mailing lists.

Subject Line: The line on an e-mail message that tells you what it's about.

Surf: A term used for browsing through the Internet and going from computer to computer on the Internet, usually without staying too long in any one place.

Text file: A file that contains only characters from the ASCII character set, with no graphics or special symbols.

Thread: A series of messages or conversations that follow a single thought or topic.

Unzipping: A software system that allows compressed files to be downloaded and then expanded to their original size and capability.

Upload: To send information from your computer to a remote computer on the Internet.

URL Universal Resource Locator: Another name for a web address.

Usenet: A bulletin board network system, linked to the Internet, which houses popular special interest newsgroups.

Virus: A software application designed to infect existing software and cause damage.

World Wide Web: A network within the larger network of the Internet system that allows users to exchange linked text, images and sounds over the Internet.

Zipping: A program that compresses information to a fraction of its size to make it travel over the Internet much faster. ⏻

Index

PRODUCT CATALOG

The 99¢ Gourmet™

Includes the basics you'll need to make sure that you eat well for less including over 120 pages of useful information to cut your food bills by 40 percent by applying guidelines to change the way you purchase and prepare the foods you eat.

Book   ISBN 978-1-891440-60-1   **$29.95**

Book Marketing for the Clueless®

Want to sell your books, CDs and DVDs for a profit? This audio/PDF CD includes databases of over 500 catalogs and outlets that market books and instructions on how to solicit your publications including how to be listed with Amazon.com for free.

Audio/Data CD+   ISBN 978-1-891440-49-6   **$24.95**

Clutterology® Getting Rid of Clutter and Getting Organized!

A complete manual on how to get organized, set up and maintain manageable filing systems, and eliminate clutter that gets in your way. Provides some of the simplest, easiest and most practical advice on how to remove the clutter from your life and get organized.

Book   ISBN 978-1-891440-62-5   **$34.95**
eBook*   ISBN 978-1-891440-71-7   **$10.00**

Clutterology® Eliminate the Clutter in Your Life and Get Organized!

Companion to the Clutterology book, the information in this 3 DVD set will help you to adapt your home and work environment to your style and attitude. Recorded in-studio and contains a combination of lecture and actual demonstrations using dozens of common implements found in stores to organize, clean, and reduce clutter.

DVD   ISBN 978-1-891440-61-8   **$39.95**

Highlights of Clutterology®

This audio CD has over 60 minutes of tips, tricks, insights, and stories about getting rid of your clutter and getting organized. It's ideal for reinforcement to remind you that getting organized is a step-by-step process that you can accomplish if you take it easy and stick with it.

Audio CD+   ISBN 978-1-891440-50-2   **$19.95**

How to Become a Clutterologist™

Do label makers and shelf dividers make you smile? Use your aptitude for organization to change lives and turn your decluttering skills into a moneymaking career; become a professional organizer! Includes the tools and knowledge you need to succeed in the professional organizer industry: organizing specialties, understanding the Clutter-Hoarding Scale, how to structure your business for SUCCESS, business licensing and insurance.

Book   ISBN 978-1-891440-56-4   **$29.95**
eBook*   ISBN 978-1-891440-68-7   **$10.00**

Contracts and Agreements for Inventors

Two dozen of the most utilized agreements to help ensure that what's yours stays yours. With the help of an attorney, they contain everything you'll need from a confidentiality agreement to work-for-hire agreements, assignment of rights, and partnership agreements. Comes with instructions for usage, filling out, and filing where applicable.

Data CD+   **$19.95**

**All eBooks contain a complete book in PDF format on a single CD for use on Macintosh and Windows computers.*
+*All data files are in PDF format, playable/viewable on Windows and Mac, audio files are in Wave format playable on standard CD players.*

E-Publishing for the Clueless®

Looking for information about how to create an eBook? Want to get your books and products on Amazon.com or listed as paid downloads on Kindle™ or the new iPAD™? Learn, step-by-step, how to create eBooks for literally *nothing*. Plus, how to publish a book with up to 64 pgs and a gloss cover for less than 50 cents per book!

Book and Windows Software CD   ISBN 978-1-8911440-72-4   **$39.95**

Fishin' With A Net

Learn the elements of designing a Web site that actually works for you and can be created in less than four hours. Covers what the Web really is, what to put on your site to be successful, and how to link with the search engines quickly and easily.

Book   ISBN 978-1-891440-55-7   **$24.95**
eBook*   ISBN 978-1-891440-42-7   **$10.00**

Goin' Pro

If you want to be a professional speaker, this program, recorded live at the Toastmasters International Convention will show you three ways you make money in the speaking business: how to work for seminar companies, ways to market yourself and how to create written products for back-of-room sales.

DVD   **$19.95**

Headline Creator™ Pro Suite

"Your headline can result in 80 percent or more of the effectiveness of your ad or sales page!" Automatically generates time-tested, proven, results-oriented headlines based on the greatest headlines in history...and does it in 17 seconds!

Windows Software CD   **$19.95**

Home Business Tax Savings Made Easy!

The average home business owner is overpaying taxes by at least $20.00 a day because of what they don't know. You'll learn the big tax breaks available to home-based business owners, exactly how to qualify for each of them, and how to easily keep bullet-proof tax records.

Book   ISBN 0-9707538-9-6   **$37.00**

How to Develop an Effective Web Site

Self-running CD takes you through the process of creating Web sites and getting them posted on the Web. Includes over 130 narrated slides with complete details and explanations on everything from renting a domain name cheaply to getting a shopping cart for FREE!

Data CD[+]   ISBN 978-1-891440-43-4   **$19.95**

How To Sell Your Inventions for Cash

Everything you need to know to be a successful inventor! Takes your idea from inception through the licensing process to a manufacturer for royalties. Learn how to protect your inventions using patents, trademarks, copyrights, and other legal instruments, determine if you're ready to offer your idea, and how to find and solicit manufacturers who are interested in your ideas.

Book   ISBN 978-1-891440-27-4   **$24.95**
eBook*   ISBN 978-1-891440-69-4   **$10.00**
Audio CD[+]   ISBN 978-1-891440-28-1   **$39.95**

Intellectual Property Protection for the Clueless®

CD contains 3 hours of audio plus 100s of pages in PDF format on trademarks, patents and copyright. Includes forms for filing without an attorney! *Bonus: How to Apply for an Innovation Research Grant!* This audio is in MP3 format playable with the Widows Media Player or comparable MP3 software.

MP3 Audio/Data CD[+]   ISBN 978-1-891440-67-0   **$59.95**

---

*All eBooks contain a complete book in PDF format on a single CD for use on Macintosh and Windows computers.
+All data files are in PDF format, playable/viewable on Windows and Mac, audio files are in Wave format playable on standard CD players.

Marketing for the Clueless®

The process of successful marketing is mechanics – not magic, and the mechanics have been simply explained to apply to all your needs. You'll learn the seven elements of marketing, how they apply to you and how to create a marketing plan that actually works for you.

Audio/Data CD⁺   ISBN 978-1-891440-54-0   **$24.95**

Marketing the One-Person Business

A one-person business is different from any other because you have to do the business PLUS get the business. Contains complete information about setup, operation, independent contractor criteria and forms, fee setting, consulting, public speaking, seminars, contracts and agreements.

Book   ISBN 978-1-891440-29-8   **$24.95**
eBook*   ISBN 978-1-891440-41-0   **$10.00**

Marketing with Postcards

The most cost effective way to promote any product or service is with postcards. You'll learn how to design a GOOD marketing postcard that gets response, how to effectively evaluate your postcards before printing, and resources for low-cost postcard layout and printing.

DVD   ISBN 978-1-891440-34-2   **$39.95**

Mechanics of Starting a Home-Based Business

A home-based business is a business whose primary office is in the owner's home. Explains the realities of starting and operating a home business and including resources for taxes, licenses, and advertising plus computer operated business you can start and run.

Book   ISBN 978-1-891440-63-2   **$34.95**
eBook*   ISBN 978-1-891440-70-0   **$10.00**

Mining the College Market

Local colleges provide hundreds of millions of dollars in revenues each year and are responsible for well over 200,000 paid training programs each year. Contains a 212 page manual with complete resources plus a three hour seminar on auto run CD, complete with narrative and slides plus a special edition of Self Publishing for the Clueless®.

Book and CD⁺   **$399.00**

Missing Tools Software Suite

Web site add-ons: Site search engine, Misspelling Generator that creates misspelled keywords to help overcome inability of searchers to correctly spell your meta-tags, Thumbnail Tool provides batch thumbnailing for images, and Slideshow Maker converts multiple views and turns still images into a self-running slide show presentation.

Windows Software CD   **$79.95**

Name Razor™

The ultimate naming software utility that uses a database of hundreds of *namelets*, to quickly create thousands of potential name ideas in minutes! It'll help you with domain names, company name, info products, brands... and more.

Windows Software CD   **$19.95**

Photo Manipulator Pro

Shrink Pic™ software automatically reduces the size of photos for email, blogging and web galleries. No set up, no operating instructions, just send your photos normally and Shrink Pic™ does the work. Paint Shop Pro™ 4 is an easy to use photo editing program that let's you enhance your photos and create professional-looking images.

Windows Software CD   **$19.95**

Professional Speaking for the Clueless®

Do you want to be paid to speak? Explains the REAL business of professional speaking and how to make six figures a year without huge marketing and advertising costs. Includes dozens of resources, databases, and complete explanations of how to locate speaking opportunities and market to them.

Audio/Data CD[+]   ISBN 978-1-891440-53-3   **$24.95**

Profitable Publishing for the Clueless®

The complete 3 CD set containing everything you need to know to generate, protect, and market your printed work. See full description for each item.

Disk 1 - Self-Publishing for the Clueless®
Disk 2 - Trademarks & Copyrights for the Clueless®
Disk 3 - Book Marketing for the Clueless®

Audio/Data CD[+]   ISBN 978-1-891440-51-9   **$59.95**

Project Management for the Clueless®

Organizing and managing projects doesn't have to be complicated and effective project management doesn't take a long time to learn – just a simple explanation of what needs to be done and why! This CD will show you how to organize, budget, and manage projects in three hours or less.

Audio/Data CD[+]   ISBN 978-1-891440-37-3   **$24.95**

Self-Publishing for the Clueless®

You can write and publish your own book for less than $3.00 per copy, in less than 90 days. Contains complete information, examples, and resources for everything you'll need including get bar codes, cover designs, and low-cost printing sources.

Audio/Data CD[+]   ISBN 978-1-891440-36-6   **$24.95**

Speakers/Publishers Support Material

Contains software including Acoustica™, Audacity™ Audio Recorders, Label Maker, PDF software and Microsoft Producer®. Comes complete with narration and special effects and a Tips Booklet Template® that can be used as a cut and paste model for your own tips booklet.

Windows Software and Data CD   **$39.95**

Talk, Talk, Talk

A 2½ hour DVD that shows you how to speak for free and make money on the luncheon circuit, present seminars and workshops at local colleges and how to get on talk radio shows sell products and promote yourself into a nationally recognized expert.

DVD   ISBN 978-1-891440-48-9   **$39.95**

Trademarks & Copyrights for the Clueless®

Trademarks are the mark of your trade and Copyrights address the laws allowing you the rights to make copies of your work. Contains printable forms and examples, explaining how to protect your works plus what material of others you can use without fear of legal problems.

Audio/Data CD[+]   ISBN 978-1-891440-30-4   **$24.95**

Venture Capital for the Clueless®

Venture capital is available for all types of businesses and your ability to tap into it depends on your ability to write a business plan that sells you and your ideas to the people with the money. Includes explanations, samples, printable forms, and sources of venture funding.

Audio/Data CD[+]   ISBN 978-1-891440-31-1   **$24.95**

---

*All eBooks contain a complete book in PDF format on a single CD for use on Macintosh and Windows computers.
+All data files are in PDF format, playable/viewable on Windows and Mac, audio files are in Wave format playable on standard CD players.

VideoWeb Wizard™

Software suite to convert your audio and video recordings to Flash™ format for fast and efficient downloads of audio and video on your Web site. Includes VideoWeb Wizard™ software and tutorial, Flash Audio Wizard™, Audacity™ Audio Recording and Editing software plus bonus programs.

Windows Software CD **$99.95**

Whadda We Do NOW?™

Provides quick fixes for failing businesses. Learn how to quickly and easily figure out what's wrong so you can stop guessing and start implementing solutions. The information is practical, easy to understand, and readily implementable if you're serious about getting your business into a positive cash flow position-NOW!

Book ISBN 978-1-891440-66-3 **$29.95**

Training Kits

Become a Professional Organizer

If you'd like to get into the lucrative world of professional organizing, then everything you'll need to setup a business, get clients, and operate profitably is on the list below. Contains:

Books: How to Become a Clutterologist™, Clutterology® Getting Rid of Clutter and Getting Organized! Mechanics of Starting a Home-Based Business, and Marketing the One-Person Business.

Plus DVD/CDs: Headline Creator™ Pro Suite, How to Develop an Effective Web Site, Marketing with Postcards, Profitable Publishing for the Clueless®, and Clutterology® Eliminate the Clutter in Your Life and Get Organized!

Kit **$261.95**

Entrepreneurship

Do you dream of working for yourself? This kit includes everything for setting up a home based business, getting organized, raising venture capital to fund the efforts, scheduling and managing your time, and ways to market your skills profitably. Contains:

Books: Mechanics of Starting a Home-Based Business, Marketing the One-Person Business, Clutterology® Getting Rid of Clutter and Getting Organized! and How to Develop an Effective Web Site.

Plus DVD/CDs: Headline Creator™ Pro Suite, Speakers/Publishers Support Materials, Marketing with Postcards, Project Management for the Clueless®, Marketing for the Clueless®, Professional Speaking for the Clueless®, Profitable Publishing for the Clueless®, and Venture Capital for the Clueless®.

Kit **$169.95**

Invention Marketing

The material listed is endorsed by the SBA as "The only legitimate program for marketing inventions that we've ever seen." It explains how to organize and manage your invention process, protect them with patents, trademarks and copyrights, set up a home business, offer your ideas for sale, plus information for raising venture capital to fund your projects. Contains:

Books: How to Sell Your Inventions for Cash and Mechanics of Starting a Home-Based Business.

Plus DVD/CDs: How to Sell Your Inventions for Cash, Contracts and Agreements for Inventors, Venture Capital for the Clueless®, Project Management for the Clueless®, and Trademarks & Copyrights for the Clueless®.

Kit **$161.95**

Marketing

Your business has two parts: getting the business and doing the business. If you're like most people, you're probably very good at doing the business but unsure about being able to get the business. This kit of materials will help you get past the problems of "getting" the business including materials for creating headlines, writing advertising copy, and locating low-cost, high profit ways to promote your business. Contains:

Book: Marketing the One-Person Business.

Plus DVD/CDs: Marketing for the Clueless®, Profitable Publishing for the Clueless®, Marketing with Postcards, Headline Creator™ Pro Suite, and How to Develop an Effective Web Site.

Kit **$191.95**

All eBooks contain a complete book in PDF format on a single CD for use on Macintosh and Windows computers.
+*All data files are in PDF format, playable/viewable on Windows and Mac, audio files are in Wave format playable on standard CD players.*

Professional Speaking

If you're interested in professional speaking, you'll find everything needed to get profitable bookings including places to get booked and instructions on how to do it! Includes over 1,700 pages of printable information, eight hours of video, four hours of audio, and hundreds of support resources. Contains:

Books: Mining the College Market (plus CDs), Marketing the One-Person Business, Mechanics of Starting A Home-Based Business, andFishin' with a Net.

Plus DVD/CDs: Headline Creator™ Pro Suite, Speakers/Publishers Support Material, Marketing with Postcards, Talk, Talk, Talk, Project Management for the Clueless®, Marketing for the Clueless®, Professional Speaking for the Clueless®, and Profitable Publishing for the Clueless®.

Kit $261.95

Raising Venture Capital

Looking for money or backing for a new idea or enterprise? Confused about what to do and how to approach investors? We've assembled the materials needed to establish proprietary rights to your innovations; plan, budget, organize and schedule your project; prepare a business plan and shop it to people with investment capital. Contains:

Books: Clutterology® Getting Rid of Clutter and Getting Organized! and Mechanics of Starting a Home-Based Business.

Plus DVD/CDs: Trademarks & Copyrights for the Clueless®, Venture Capital for the Clueless®, Project Management for the Clueless®, Marketing for the Clueless®, Profitable Publishing for the Clueless®, Headline Creator™ Pro Suite, How to Develop an Effective Web Site, Marketing with Postcards, Clutterology® Eliminate the Clutter in Your Life and Get Organized!

Kit $191.95

Self-Publishing

You CAN have a book ready to sell in 30 days with these practical products...guaranteed! Contains everything needed including pre-configured scheduling and budgeting charts to get your own project finished in record time with a minimal amount of expense and hassles. Contains:

Books: Mechanics of Starting A Home-Based Business, and Fishin' With A Net.

Plus DVD/CDs: Self-Publishing for the Clueless®, Trademarks & Copyrights for the Clueless®, Book Marketing for the Clueless®, Marketing for the Clueless®, Headline Creator™ Pro Suite, Marketing with Postcards, and Project Management for the Clueless®.

Kit $261.95

Web Site Development Software Suite

No software you use to create your Web site will contain everything you need, so we've assembled the "stuff they left out." This suite of software and resources will help make your Web site work efficiently and get the response it deserves. These products have a proven track record in the world of Web design, marketing and advertising. Contains:

DVD/CDs: Video Web Wizard™, Flash Audio Web Wizard™, Headline Creator™ Pro Suite, Marketing With Postcards, Zoom-Your own Site Search Engine, Typo-Misspelling Generator, Image Thumbnail Resizer and Flash Slideshow Maker.

Kit $100.00

All eBooks contain a complete book in PDF format on a single CD for use on Macintosh and Windows computers.
+All data files are in PDF format, playable/viewable on Windows and Mac, audio files are in Wave format playable on standard CD players.

"Business and Technology Training Specialists"

6318 Ridgepath Court • Rancho Palos Verdes, CA 90275-3248
Telephone: (310) 544-9502 Fax (310) 544-3017 • www.RoundsMiller.com

ORDER FORM

ITEM (See Catalog for Full Description)	Format	Qty.	Price
The 99¢ Gourmet™	Book $29.95		
Book Marketing for the Clueless®	Audio/Data CD $24.95		
Clutterology® Getting Rid of Clutter and Getting Organized!	Book $34.95		
	eBook $10.00		
Clutterology® Eliminate the Clutter in Your Life and Get Organized!	DVD $39.95		
Highlights of Clutterology®	Audio CD $19.95		
How to Become a Clutterologist™	Book $29.95		
	eBook $10.00		
Contracts and Agreements for Inventors	Data CD $19.95		
E-Publishing for the Clueless®	Book/Software CD $39.95		
Fishin' With A Net	Book $24.95		
	eBook $10.00		
Goin' Pro	DVD $19.95		
Headline Creator™ Pro Suite	Software CD $19.95		
Home Business Tax Savings Made Easy!	Book $37.00		
How to Develop an Effective Web Site	Data CD $19.95		
How To Sell Your Inventions for Cash	Book $24.95		
	eBook $10.00		
	Audio CD $39.95		
Intellectual Property Protection for the Clueless®	MP3 Audio/Data CD $59.95		
Marketing for the Clueless®	Audio/Data CD $24.95		
Marketing the One-Person Business	Book $24.95		
	eBook $10.00		
Marketing with Postcards	DVD $39.95		
Mechanics of Starting a Home-Based Business	Book $34.95		
	eBook $10.00		
Mining the College Market	Book and CD $399.00		
Missing Tools Software Suite	Software CD $79.95		
Name Razor™	Software CD $19.95		
Photo Manipulator Software	Software CD $19.95		
Professional Speaking for the Clueless®	Audio/Data CD $24.95		
Profitable Publishing for the Clueless®	Audio/Data CD $59.95		
Project Management for the Clueless®	Audio/Data CD $24.95		
Self-Publishing for the Clueless®	Audio/Data CD $24.95		
Speakers/Publishers Support Material	Software/Data CD $39.95		
Talk, Talk, Talk	DVD $39.95		
Trademarks & Copyrights for the Clueless®	Audio/Data CD $24.95		
Venture Capital for the Clueless®	Audio/Data CD $24.95		

Page 1   Sub-Total

VideoWeb Wizard™	*Software CD $99.95*		
Whadda We Do NOW?™	*Book $29.95*		
Become a Professional Organizer	*Kit $261.95*		
Entrepreneurship	*Kit $169.95*		
Invention Marketing	*Kit $161.95*		
Marketing	*Kit $191.95*		
Professional Speaking	*Kit $261.95*		
Raising Venture Capital	*Kit $191.95*		
Self-Publishing	*Kit $261.95*		
Web Site Development Software Suite	*Kit $100.00*		

Thank You!

Amount from Page 1	
Sub-Total	
in CA add Sales Tax 9.75%	
Shipping	**$2.95**
Total	

Name (please print) _____

Mailing Address: _____

City, State, ZIP: _____

Tel: _____ e-Mail: _____

I authorize Rounds, Miller and Associates to charge my credit card for the items listed above

Credit Card Number: _____ exp. _____ CSS_____

Signature: _____ Date: _____

(If different than above)

Name on Card:_____

Statement Address: _____

City, State, ZIP: _____

To Order By Mail:

Send completed order form and check payable to Rounds, Miller and Associates to

6318 Ridgepath Court

Rancho Palos Verdes, CA 90275

To Order By Fax:

Fax both pages of completed order form with credit card info to Rounds, Miller and Associates

Fax (310) 544-3017